HOW TO TALK
TO YOUR BOSS
ABOUT RACE

HOW TO TALK TO YOUR BOSS ABOUT RACE

Speaking Up Without Getting Shut Down

Y-VONNE HUTCHINSON

PORTFOLIO / PENGUIN

Portfolio/Penguin
An imprint of Penguin Random House LLC
penguinrandomhouse.com

Most Portfolio books are available at a discount when purchased in quantity for sales
promotions or corporate use. Special editions, which include personalized covers,
excerpts, and corporate imprints, can be created when purchased in large
quantities. For more information, please call (212) 572-2232 or email
specialmarkets@penguinrandomhouse.com. Your local bookstore can also
assist with discounted bulk purchases using the Penguin Random House
corporate Business-to-Business program. For assistance in locating
a participating retailer, email B2B@penguinrandomhouse.com.

Graphic on page 85 adapted from graphic by Josh Kahn via CC BY-NC-SA 4.0
(creativecommons.org/licenses/by-nc-sa/4.0/legalcode); chart on page 91
adapted from chart by the Change Agency via CC BY-NC-SA 4.0
(creativecommons.org/licenses/by-nc-sa/4.0/legalcode).

Library of Congress Cataloging-in-Publication Data
Names: Hutchinson, Y-Vonne, author.
Title: How to talk to your boss about race : speaking up
without getting shut down / Y-Vonne Hutchinson.
Description: New York : Portfolio/Penguin, [2022] |
Includes bibliographical references.
Identifiers: LCCN 2021031583 (print) | LCCN 2021031584 (ebook) |
ISBN 9780593418093 (hardcover) | ISBN 9780593421147 (ebook)
Subjects: LCSH: Diversity in the workplace—United States. |
Racism—United States. | Discrimination in employment—United States. |
Organizational behavior—United States.
Classification: LCC HF5549.5.M5 H88 2022 (print) |
LCC HF5549.5.M5 (ebook) | DDC 658.3008—dc23
LC record available at https://lccn.loc.gov/2021031583
LC ebook record available at https://lccn.loc.gov/2021031584

Printed in the United States of America
1st Printing

BOOK DESIGN BY MEIGHAN CAVANAUGH

*To Mom, the older I get the more magical,
powerful I realize you are.*

To Dad, for showing me how to prove them wrong.

To Kia, the living embodiment of quiet strength.

*To Justin, for being a true loving partner in every sense
of the word. None of this works without you.*

To my beautiful daughter, for changing the game.

*To the friends, colleagues, and mentors who
supported me along the way.*

*And most of all, to Nita. Our reunion was cut short;
but your love, your sweetness, your humor, and your
dedication live on. My God, how I wish you were here.*

CONTENTS

PREFACE

Let's cut the bullshit.

Racism is real. It's profound. It touches all of us, no matter what color our skin is. If you've spent any time alive in this country, or in this world, you know this.

So what are you supposed to do about it? Since the mass outrage in response to the killing of George Floyd, protestors have taken to the streets (and to Instagram) to raise awareness about racism and demand action from the institutions that police us, govern us, and lead us. Cities defunded their police departments. And it is no longer controversial to say "Black Lives Matter."

But we've also seen backlash. Some of that police funding came back. Racially motivated hate crimes against Black and Asian people have dramatically increased. Some states have even started cracking down on the way we teach about racism and our history in schools, panicking over critical race theory.

You might be one of those protesters. You might be worried about the backlash. You might have read *How to Be an Antiracist* and *White Fragility*. Heck, maybe you even have a whole book club. You now know that racism still exists and you're committed to creating antiracist change. And now you're stuck.

That's where I come in.

I run ReadySet, a diversity consulting and strategy firm that works with Fortune 500 companies, the entertainment industry, tech companies, nonprofits, and government bodies to help them become more diverse, equitable, and inclusive. When it comes to also making them antiracist? Let's just say we're working hard and we have a long way to go.

If you are truly committed to antiracism, arguably nowhere is more important than your workplace, the place where you spend the majority of your waking hours and the institution where you have the most power to create change. Yes—*you* have power. Even if you're in a support role, instead of in the C-suite. Even if you're an executive assistant, not the chief executive officer.

This book does what it says—it teaches you how to talk to your boss about race and racism. You'll learn how to find your allies, how to recognize and make the most of your power within your organization, and how to prepare for your conversation to make it as effective as possible. I'll give you the prompts and one-liners that have worked best for me, and real talk about when, maybe, you should just walk away from your toxic workplace (and how to do it without burning bridges—or, how to explode them magnificently and publicly, if that's what you want).

In many ways, this book is a product of its time: the rise of the whistle-blower, the surge of interest in systemic racism, accelerated economic equality, the unequal trauma of the pandemic that hurt people of color disproportionately, and the global rise in racist violence.

That is where we are now.

But this book is also timeless. Racism has existed for centuries. It was a foundational organizing principle of the United States, the country I'm from. It restricts opportunities for people around the world. Our identities have always determined where we've been able to work comfortably. Potential has always been equitably distributed, while opportunity has not. That is the way things have always been.

But that could change. We can change it. Maybe everything that's happened—the killings, the outrage, the events that we've lived through while I wrote this book, and the pain we've all had to navigate since then—could be just the catalyst we need.

I hope this book becomes your essential guide to translating pain into action, awareness into change. I hope you see this as a handbook to return to over and over—your guide to dismantling racism in the place where you spend most of your time. This book was written to help you navigate a conversation with your boss, but I hope that you use it for more than just that. The frameworks I introduce and the techniques we discuss can inform your antiracist work elsewhere, from the dinner table to your next PTA meeting. Wherever you are, there's someone you need to talk to about race.

I would argue the thing that racism does most effectively, aside from killing people and draining generations' worth of collective potential, is waste time. I wasted my time trying to be the perfect Black person. I wasted my time trying to fix something that was never broken. I wasted my time trying to avoid racism instead of fighting it head-on. I wasted my time thinking there could be any fairness for people like me in the workplace without justice or repair.

I let racism waste my time, but you don't have to. I'm willing to bet you bought this book because you are sick of wasting precious time not confronting the elephant in the room. Chances are you bought it in preparation for one of the toughest conversations you will have in your career. Silence and avoidance are no longer options that you are willing to consider. I hope this book gets you closer to where you want to be as efficiently as possible. I hope this book helps you embrace your power and find your words.

MY WAKE-UP CALL

My first job was at a famous theme park in Arlington, Texas. I was fifteen. Back then, to figure out where to place you, they would have you take an aptitude test and give you a series of interviews. I was an honors student, annoyingly gregarious in the way that only a theater kid could be. I aced the exam and thought I did a pretty good job of charming my interviewers. When the time for job assignments came, I breathlessly awaited the opportunity to hop on concessions (like most kids my age), or serve as a greeter, or, if dreams really did come true, *work in costume.* Imagine my surprise when I was assigned to janitorial services.

I spent my summer cleaning bathrooms and picking up used condoms out of the bushes. I worked hard. I made money. And, trite as it may sound, I learned the value of a dollar.

But I always wondered: Why janitorial services? Why did so many of the kids who cleaned bathrooms look like me? Why did the greeters and the ticket takers look, well, so much paler?

Maybe I didn't do as well on the test as I thought. Maybe I was more annoying than gregarious. Maybe they just couldn't see me anywhere else. Maybe it was nothing.

Maybe it was something.

That job was the first of many that would leave me with lingering questions. Eventually, I would become an international human rights lawyer and labor rights advocate working in countries around the world, from Afghanistan to the Thai/Burma border to Nicaragua. Looking back, I think I left the United States to "help others" (don't get me started on the nonprofit-industrial complex) in part because I was trying to escape the racism that constrained me at home. Of course, I couldn't. After the killings of Trayvon Martin and Eric Garner and countless others, I couldn't escape the feeling that I was running away to fight someone else's fight while my people were suffering and dying at home. So I came back.

Before then, I had thought of race the same way I thought about video games: it was a challenge to be beaten and nothing else. Of course, I was wrong. There is no way out of Blackness. No number of White friends can shield you. No Ivy League school or fancy degree can save you. No job will exempt you.

I got my wake-up call, as many a Black achiever does, after entering the professional workforce. Naive idiot that I was, I saw my career as the culmination of all of my hard work, the manifestation of all of my "Black excellence." It was, in truth, the beginning of my failure.

Smart as I was, I could never quite fit into any office

environment. Hard as I worked, I never seemed to satisfy my bosses. I never got mentorship, never got guidance, was lucky to get feedback. I recently did an exercise at a workplace training where I was asked to share a story about a good manager. I struggled to come up with one. I've had quite a few managers in my day. I saw some of them who were really good with my teammates, who formed close bonds and established lifelong relationships with those they worked with. They never quite connected with me.

Early on, I thought my failure to connect and advance was because there was something wrong with me. I was too distant or too friendly. I was too focused on the work or not focused enough. I was too outspoken or maybe I was too withdrawn.

Thank God for the internet. In spite of quite a few not-great things, one thing that it has done quite well is demystify and unmask racism. It turned out that a lot of Black women had similar stories to mine. As I sought out their narratives, I started to see similar patterns. I was not the only one who'd had colleagues who told them without provocation that they were scary. It turns out many professional Black women have been asked to be less direct in their emails. And you would be shocked at just how many of us were "accidentally" left out of office social gatherings, had difficulty getting feedback on our work, or struggled to find mentors. Everyone wanted to touch our hair! We experienced the same exclusion, feelings of alienation, and difficulty advancing. While the circumstances differed, the root cause was the same: racism.

Coming to that truth was painful, but it was also liberating. There is freedom in knowing. Recognizing that I wasn't the problem—racism was—freed me from spending the rest of my career engaging in the Sisyphean task of contorting myself to an impossible standard. Realizing that I could never be perfect enough to escape that problem freed me up to do better things with my time, like learn to love who I am; fight the actual enemy, racism; and write this book.

It's no coincidence that my mystical journey of racial self-delusion ended when I entered into the professional workforce. Nowhere is the issue of race more embedded than in the workplace. In fact, I would argue that it's almost impossible to decouple the two.

The workplace has always been racially segregated,

especially in the United States. Whiteness means access to more mobility and better opportunities. While not all White people get to work cushy white-collar jobs, almost all of the cushy white-collar jobs go to White people; other racial groups are funneled into low-wage or working-class occupations with minimal labor protections. From enslaved Black people and sharecroppers to Chinese laundry workers to Mexican farmworkers, specific racial and ethnic groups have always been limited in the kinds of work that they are legally allowed to do. The American workforce was built to be segregated.

In fact, working conditions are so tied to racial identity that many of the racial stereotypes we battle today were created to justify the labor that different racial groups were expected to perform. Enslaved Africans were characterized as brutish, impervious to pain, ignorant, masculine, and hypersexualized to justify their exploitation in hard manual labor. In the late nineteenth century, during the gold rush, Chinese men were labeled as feminized and submissive in part to justify pushing them to be laundry workers and excluding them from more lucrative trades. These stereotypes still affect us inside and outside of the workplace today.

Fighting racism at work means pushing the workplace to become something that it has absolutely never been before: truly equitable. I always tell my clients, in the working world the default is exclusion, racism, sexism, and ableism. To strive for an equitable workplace is to constantly fight against the headwinds of bias and structural inequality. Many organizations fail to achieve their goals related to equity precisely because they forget this one crucial fact. To combat the pressure to return to the default, we must always proactively strive for inclusion. Otherwise, it is only a matter of time before our working environments return to inequality.

Today, the headwinds are stronger than they have ever been before. The epidemic of COVID-19 has ravaged the American workforce, disproportionally pushing out women, especially women of color.

The disease has left us traumatized. In the United States, we're grappling with the loss of more than half a million people to the disease. Those we lost were disproportionately people of color, many of whom were essential workers who did not have the luxury to stay at home. We rushed to bury them. Some of us did not get a chance to say goodbye. Some of us did not get to fully mourn.

The trauma of the epidemic has been compounded by the global rise in racist violence. Police killings of Black people and a rise in anti-Asian violence have impacted communities not just in the United States but in Europe as well.

The flip side of all this is that workers are also more empowered than they ever have been before. As I write this, the United States is experiencing a major labor shortage. Employers have 8.1 million positions open, and 10 million workers are looking for work. Yet payrolls have increased only by a few hundred thousand workers every month. This discrepancy is driven by the fact that many low-wage workers, a significant number of whom are people of color, are refusing to work in toxic environments for less-than-livable wages under dangerous working conditions. They want better—better jobs with better working conditions and better compensation.

Now is the time to push for change.

Addressing the issues will be vital to building inclusive workplace cultures in the years ahead. Accounting for the uniquely heavy burden borne by people of color in the workplace must be part of that effort.

It's a tough job, but if you don't do it, who else will?

I'm honored that at this point in your journey you've looked here for help.

Good thing too, because I wrote this book just for you.

IT ALL STARTS WITH A CONVERSATION

Antiracism at work is a journey. For many people, that journey starts with the right conversation.

Yes, that sounds hokey. And, yes, there are a lot of trash takes out there that rely way too much on conversation as a lever for change. But the truth is you can't undertake this work without strong communication, healthy collaboration, relationships, and support. And how do you get those things? Conversation.

I want to empower you to have these tough conversations well: to help you face the racism you see at work head-on, to cut through the noise and the bullshit, to position yourself and others for transformative action, and to stop wasting your time on the people who won't change.

Before we get started, I'd like to invite you to close your eyes (well, read this paragraph first, *then* close your eyes). Imagine a truly antiracist organization. Think about what it looks like. Who gets to lead? Who thrives? How do people communicate with each other? How do they support one another? What does the workplace culture celebrate? What won't it tolerate?

You can open your eyes.

Now ask yourself: What kind of transformation would it take to get there? How significant would that transformation be for you as a person of color or an ally? What are you willing to do to help make it happen?

That transformations starts with a conversation—the one you're about to have. So it's time to get you ready to have it.

Let's go.

HOW TO TALK
TO YOUR BOSS
ABOUT RACE

READING THE ROOM
SPOTTING THE SIGNS OF RACISM

Language is a challenge when it comes to the words we use to describe race and racism. It's constantly evolving to become more specific, expansive, and inclusive. It's also constantly being co-opted or weaponized to undermine its effectiveness.

Just look at what happened to the word "woke." The word comes from the phrase "Stay woke," a longtime rallying cry of the Black American civil rights movement. That cry was a reminder to Black Americans to remain aware of the injustices they faced and the dangers posed by White people. It was a warning against complacency during a time when complacency could mean death.

Consider the words of Dr. Martin Luther King Jr.:

> *There are all too many people who, in some great period of social change, fail to achieve the new mental outlooks that the new situation demands. There is nothing more tragic than to sleep through a revolution. There can be no gainsaying of the fact that a great revolution is taking place in our world today. It is a social revolution, sweeping away the old order of colonialism. And in our own nation it is sweeping away the old order of slavery and racial segregation.... And so we see in our own world a revolution of rising expectations. The great challenge facing every individual graduating today is to remain awake through this social revolution.*

Appropriately, the phrase "Stay woke" reappeared in 2014 as Black death started to fill our Twitter timelines and Black citizens took to the streets in Ferguson, Missouri. It became a rallying cry for the Black Lives Matter movement, and the hashtag #staywoke encouraged people to pay attention to the atrocities happening in Ferguson and the larger specter of impunity for officers who killed Black people.

After being featured in popular music and film, the term eventually entered the mainstream and, of course, became the source of political backlash. "Woke" became a shorthand critique of performative allyship, or just of people who were annoyingly insistent about those pesky civil rights. Today, if we're not careful, we can be tricked into engaging with "wokeness" solely on those negative terms, instead of striving for it as Dr. King asked us to.

Language is fluid. It evolves, gets appropriated, gets weaponized, is reclaimed, and on and on. Nowhere is this more true than with words and ideas that have been politicized.

With that caveat, I thought it best to start with a primer, introducing language and clarifying some of the concepts I utilize when I talk about race today.

WHAT IS RACE?

Before we define racism, we should first define race.

It would be fair to say that when it comes to defining the word "race," I am not sure how exactly to do that. It would be fairer to say that I have been wrestling with this question most of my life and I still feel like I come up short.

I know race is the thing that made all of the difference. I know it is often the first aspect of my identity that people refer to when they describe me. I know it helps me create community with some and puts me in danger with others. It is my hair, my skin, my butt, my nose, the origins of my ancestors, our history. That much I know

I also know I learned I was Black in first grade.

That year, my mother pulled me out of my small Christian private school and put me into public school. Prior to that transition, I had been sheltered (though not in the way that you might think). My private school was incredibly diverse. My mother was a substitute teacher there. I never had cause to interrogate my identity or focus on my racial difference, because no one else did either. Not so in my all-White public school, where I both stuck out like a sore thumb and seemed invisible at the same time.

I struggled to understand why things at the school I was so excited to attend felt so different . . . so much worse.

A boy named Scott helped me solve that mystery. We were on the playground doing some activity that required us to hold hands. Scott refused to hold mine because I was Black. I tried not to cry. The teacher pretended not to see. And that was the day I learned what Blackness meant.

Today, I very much know I'm Black. I'm a girl who will never pass. I'm Blackity Black Black. Society told me I was Black. My parents made sure I never forgot it. But that knowledge wasn't inherent. I wasn't born knowing it. Sure, when I was younger, I knew I was different from my White classmates. I knew my skin was darker and my hair was kinkier, just as I knew some of us had brown eyes and some of us had blue eyes. I just didn't know it was a thing that couldn't be ignored. That race was the difference that mattered. It was something that I had to be taught to see. I had to be told I was Black. I had to be taught what that meant, told the ways in which it would impact my life. Schooled on how to survive it. Admonished when I wasn't performing it correctly.

I was born knowing my father, my mother, our family, our culture. But that's different from race. Race is in the eye of the beholder. My racial identity was constructed by those around me—their reaction to me and treatment of me, and my reaction to that. My Blackness isn't static. In some countries, like Ghana, Uganda, or Nigeria, where everyone is "Black," it doesn't exist at all, or at least not in the same way it does in the United States. Blackness is relative. Race is relative, which makes it hard for me to say definitively what it is.

Luckily, smarter, far more eloquent people than I have taken a stab at defining this elusive concept.

In *How to Be an Antiracist*, Ibram X. Kendi writes that race is "a power construct of blended difference that lives socially." According to Kendi, our science, policies, ideas, and cultures animate and solidify race. Reflecting back on its original function—to justify the trading of enslaved people—he argues that race leverages difference to categorize, elevate, and exclude, all in the pursuit of power.

The elusiveness and subjectivity of race is a powerful mirage, writes Kendi, made up of the images that we have of ourselves and the images that others have of us, but not actually rooted in what really is there.

Kendi and other thinkers are not alone in emphasizing the social construction of race. Geneticists agree; many insist that race is a poor marker for the relationship between ancestry and genetics. For instance, there are more genetic similarities between some West Africans and Europeans than between West Africans and East Africans. And there is no single genetic variant that separates all Africans from all Europeans.

Because racial difference isn't itself a fact rooted in biology, there is a school of avoidant thought that says it doesn't exist, and therefore we should all ignore it so it goes away. But this is too simplistic. Race is real because we feel its effects. It affects our economic security, our physical health, our psychological well-being, and even our life span. That difference, the difference of impact, can't be ignored.

A quick note on how to refer to your fellow human beings. For some people this may be the hardest part of the conversation. What do people like to be called these days? As I said earlier, language is a moving target, but here's where I land. Generally, I call people of African descent—whether descended from enslaved people or not—"Black" with a capital "B." "Black" is always used as an adjective ("Black people"), never a noun ("Blacks"). I usually refer to people of Latin American descent as "Latino," "Latina," or "Latinx" (a gender-neutral term) to avoid centering Spanish identity as "Hispanic" does. "Latinx" is not used as widely in Latin American communities as Latino/a terminology, but I agree with those who argue that the term's gender-neutral framing makes it more inclusive of those with nonbinary gender identities. Occasionally, I'll use the term "BIPOC" to refer to Black and Indigenous and other people of color (POC) to highlight the distinct experiences of Black and Native people of color.

WHAT IS RACISM?

"Racial bias," "racial divisiveness," "unconscious bias," "controversial opinions," "diversity of thought"—there are a lot of euphemisms that we use for racism at work.

It's sometimes a struggle to get my clients to even say the word "race." Until recently, for most of my clients, whether executives or heads of human resources, saying the actual word "racism" seemed almost impossible.

In our consultation calls, they would so eloquently

tell me about the struggle that (White) women in their organization faced, the depths of their own unconscious bias that they had explored, their need for representation across the spectrum "in terms of gender, age, socioeconomic status, and..." There was always a pause here. It's a pretty awkward pause—hard for me, necessary for them. Sometimes, I'd want to scream out the word, just so we could move on. But of course, I couldn't do that. Acknowledging a thing exists is the first step. In any case, there would be a pause. Then they would rush through or mumble the word "race." For the vast majority of these people, who were White and South or East Asian, highly educated, and predominantly liberal, and who tended to work in organizations where most people looked like them, race felt taboo to acknowledge, and racism seemed like much too serious an allegation to even name.

Of course, after we started working together, when I spoke to the other Black and Brown employees who worked at these companies about their experiences, they had no problem saying the word. For them, racism wasn't a taboo construct but a real aspect of their daily lives that impacted the way they navigated their workplaces.

This divergence is understandable. It can be hard to identify racism at work because we struggle to define it generally. There are those of us who know it because we experience it. There are some who still believe that racism is real only if it involves a burning cross, a white hood, or a "Whites only" sign. There are those who think of racism as a rare interpersonal issue caused by a few bad apples.

Like many popular theorists, for the purposes of this book, I define racism as prejudice against someone because of their race, reinforced by systems of power.

I'd also like to go one step further here and bring in elements of critical race theory. Critical race theory is the most recent antiracist concept to face demonization and backlash; as of June 2021, Idaho, Oklahoma, North Carolina, and Tennessee have all banned teachers from teaching critical race theory in their classrooms. It's a lightning rod.

But I don't just like critical race theory because it's *edgy*. I like it because it's *accurate*.

Developed in the 1970s and 1980s by legal academics as a way to examine from a legal and policy perspective the ways in which race and institutionalized racism perpetuate racial inequality, critical race theory recognizes that race is socially constructed, and that racism is an ordinary part of everyday life. It also reminds us that racism is codified into our laws and organizations, even the ones that may appear at first glance to be neutral.

Critical race theory scares people because it acknowledges not only that racism is structural, as the "prejudice plus power" framing indicates, it is also so endemic to our society that it is our default way of operating. It discourages blind faith in institutions and encourages us to deeply examine the rules and systems that we take for granted. It insists that we can ensure change only through race-conscious antiracist mechanisms.

So, ultimately, we can say that *racism is the system of race-based preference, expressed interpersonally or institutionally, backed by political, social, cultural, and economic power, which is also embedded into our rules and institutions.*

I find this definition of racism useful, especially in the workplace, because it acknowledges the historical racist influences embedded in our labor market and American corporate culture and connects it to our broader social condition. For example, the universities we graduate from (if we get the chance to go to college at all) and the degrees we earn greatly influence our job prospects. But university admissions are incredibly biased, determined by class, economic privilege, and access to good tertiary education—and all of these factors, of course, are greatly influenced by race. Those who are able to overcome the barriers go on to face bias within their own university programs, where they may be less likely to receive mentorship or may even be discouraged from pursuing their chosen area of study.

This definition identifies racism as both personal and institutional, something that until recently many of my clients have struggled to accept. Most importantly, it helps to explain why well-intentioned companies that aren't *actively* racist can still see racist outcomes, since racism is the default. It forces us to reckon with our history, and it doesn't leave room for acontextual analysis.

If you are a White person reading this book and you have an urge to radically reimagine this definition of racism, on your own, and perhaps run that definition by the Black and Brown folks in your life without doing any research, I implore you: Please do not do that. Instead ask yourself, *Why*? What makes you uncomfortable about this definition? What parts of it do you resist? What would you embrace instead? The work that you need to do may lie in the answers to these questions.

You see, White people have been defining racism for POC since before it became bad to be racist. They have also been resisting definitions of racism that might implicate them or their interests in maintaining (or ignoring) racist systems. We can't do that here—not if we're going to tackle the racism all around us. While no one is perfect, we can't start by being part of the problem.

UNDERSTANDING THE SPECTRUM OF RACISM

It's one thing to read a definition of racism in a book, and quite another to know if you currently work in an environment that is racist. Discriminating based on race at work is illegal, so most individuals at companies know to avoid overt, public acts of racial discrimination. And individuals personally invested in ignoring racism, maybe to make themselves feel better, engage in racial gaslighting, derail discussions about racism, and downplay the impact of racism, all of which can leave you doubting whether your experiences were actually the result of racism. So how can we be certain that the people and institutions we interact with are actually racist?

That's the wrong question to ask.

Instead, shift your focus away from intent and toward impact. Focusing on intent and certainty demands that we make sure we know what's in the heart of those persons or institutions that engage in a potentially racist action before deciding on an appropriate response. That standard asks us to judge their character instead of what they have done. Of course, in most contexts, such judgment is impossible. And I would argue that the impossibility of this requirement is not accidental. Racists benefit from us wasting our time and energy trying to figure out if they actually mean to be racist. Someone tells a racist joke, and we worry about whether or not they meant to be malicious or knew their behavior could be hurtful instead of repairing the damage done and making sure it never happens again. Focusing on intent keeps us occupied while racists get to continue being racist.

Further, by placing the person engaging in racism at the center of the conversation, focusing on intent also allows those engaging in racist actions to benefit from the privileges associated with their identity, while pushing the less privileged person at the receiving end of their racism further to the margins. For example, I've seen White women accused of racism use their femininity, and the presumption of innocence associated with it, to claim ignorance of their actions or derail difficult conversations with emotional reactions. Meanwhile, the damage they inflict on their counterparts of color is ignored.

Conversely, a focus on impact acknowledges that it's difficult and counterproductive to ascertain intent. Instead, we can look at the action perpetrated by the person or institution and the harm that it caused. Instead of centering the privileged, this perspective centers the experience of the marginalized. A focus on impact sets us up much better to move toward a constructive discussion of solutions that address the harm, as opposed to frustrating circular conversations around intent.

Finally, if we accept the definition of racism offered earlier in this chapter, then we must acknowledge that rules, systems, and actions can have racism embedded within them even if they seem neutral on their face.

Taking these circumstances into account, racism can manifest in several ways.

MICROAGGRESSIONS

Originally coined by Harvard psychiatrist Dr. Chester M. Pierce and popularized by Dr. Derald Wing Sue, the term "microaggressions" refers to the small, everyday slights, intentional or unintentional, that remind those from marginalized groups that they are different. These slights can take the form of offhand comments, jokes, backhanded compliments, or insults.

In the workplace, microaggressions can look like comparing "tans" with a Black employee, mistaking a Latinx manager for custodial staff, critiquing a traditional hairstyle of an Indigenous American employee, or complimenting an Asian employee for their English-speaking ability. For me, one example of a workplace microaggression that really sticks out in my mind happened about ten years ago at a former job. I usually wear an Afro or braids. One week, I straightened my hair. My boss went to great pains to compliment it, exclaiming, "Oh my gosh! It looks so clean!"

Microaggressions are challenging to handle because of their subtlety. They are easy for targets to question, bystanders to ignore, and perpetrators to deny.

Like the concepts of unconscious bias and antiracism, microaggressions have been having a bit of a moment as people embrace this new framework for thinking about the spectrum of racist behaviors they encounter every day. There are some scholars, like Ibram X. Kendi, who bristle at the newfound embrace of this concept, insisting that it takes the edge off racism. I find the concept helpful as I encourage people to think about the spectrum of racism and reckon with the totality of racism in all its forms. Sure, we might diminish the impact of microaggressions by labeling them "micro," but there is also a risk that we might overindex on a singular manifestation of racism (as many have with unconscious bias and extreme, overt acts of racism) and forget that racism, like the self, contains multitudes.

Often referred to as "death by a thousand cuts," the harm caused by microaggressions can be just as psychologically and physiologically damaging as experiences of overt racism. For me it meant spending years damaging my hair to straighten it with heat and relaxers. But in other cases, the consequences can be far more serious. Racial microaggressions have been linked to suicidal ideation, depression, elevated risk of heart disease, diabetes, hypertension, and infectious disease.

UNCONSCIOUS BIAS

Unconscious bias refers to the bias that we all hold, informed by social stereotypes, about various identity groups. These biases unconsciously manifest in discriminatory behavior as our brains take cognitive shortcuts.

Nothing gets under my skin like a conversation about unconscious bias. I really fucking hate it. I have a whole *unconscious bias rant*. I won't write it out in full here, because I want you to learn and not just bathe in my rage. But the short version is that unconscious bias is the easy way out. It's bias without culpability. Ahistorical bias. Bias that we all have and need to look deep in our hearts to fix (but not really do anything else about). Ninety percent of the time, a conversation about unconscious bias

really needs to be a conversation about something else—
usually racism.

When we attribute racism to unconscious bias, we al-
leviate the personal responsibility of those who hold it,
maintain focus on the intent of the person holding the
bias, and fail to acknowledge the role of power in perpet-
uating bias. And there's no way to combat unconscious
bias other than to increase our awareness of it. Unfortunately, the concept has received disproportionate attention over the past few years, entering the popular lexicon
and often serving as a catchall term for all kinds of discrimination. People often say "unconscious bias" when
what they really mean is interpersonal bias or interpersonal racism. It helps soften the blow—which is another
thing we won't be doing here.

That said, the term does still serve a purpose, and I
would be remiss not to include it here. The unconscious
bias framework is useful in that it takes the taboo away
from having bias, making it easier to start conversations
about bias with less defensiveness. The framework also offers the opportunity to discuss interesting cognitive biases
that are influenced by racist beliefs. For example, we can

hold stereotypes, blanket beliefs about people because of their identity. We can have competency bias, which is the assumption that some groups of people are more competent than others, or leniency bias, which is the willingness to give certain people the benefit of the doubt while expecting more from others. Naming these specific kinds of cognitive biases can help us as bystanders recognize them when they do occur, and help us catch ourselves when we may be perpetrating them.

INTERPERSONAL RACISM

Interpersonal racism refers to the racist interactions that occur between people because of an individual's racist beliefs, biases, assumptions, or actions.

Interpersonal racism encompasses a spectrum of behavior. It can be overt or subtle. It can be conscious or unconscious. It can take the form of microaggressions or just plain aggression. It can happen with just one other person or with a group of people.

At work, interpersonal racism can manifest as outright harassment; rude and derogatory behavior; offensive jokes or comments; distancing and social exclusion; habitual failure to make eye contact or smile; ignoring or talking over colleagues; blocking opportunities for hire, promotion, or advancement; or relegating an employee to menial tasks.

Bias and racism are not the same thing. A bias refers to a preferential or an adverse response to a person as a result of aspects of their identity, including but not limited to their race. Racism refers to the personal belief that some races are superior to others. Bias can be about a lot of things—race, gender identity, disability, age, socioeconomic background. Racism is just about race.

STRUCTURAL RACISM

Structural racism refers to the system of policies, cultural practices, institutions, and ideologies that work together to create and reinforce racism. Structural racism endures over time regardless of individual action or intent. These policies, practices, and institutions may on their face appear to be neutral, but in practice result in worse outcomes for marginalized people of color. Examples of structural racism include differential public-school funding, redlining and residential segregation, and the school-to-prison pipeline.

Structural racism also manifests in the workplace. Hiring practices like in-network hiring and referrals introduce and solidify racial disparities. A preference for a strong "culture fit" tends to disproportionately impact those from underrepresented racial groups, who may be seen as outsiders. And in many places, a glass ceiling exists for Black and Brown people, who are kept out of positions of leadership.

The workplace has been historically racist—racially segregated, racially segmented, and racially biased. Access to certain types of work has been considered a privilege, and relegation to other, less prestigious types of work has to be justified through racist beliefs about non-White groups' worth as human beings. In the history of the United States, Black people were enslaved and White people were anything but. White women were house-wives, and women of color were used for domestic labor and childcare. Even today, doctors, engineers, and scientists are stereotyped as White and South or East Asian.

The C-suite is White; administrative staff and janitorial services aren't.

The workplace also interacts with many other racist systems and institutions to reinforce racist outcomes. Our systems of education, transportation, and housing all affect our access to work. Systems of lending, access to capital, and mentorship affect who owns, operates, and leads businesses and therefore the culture and practices of the workplace.

At work, structural racism may result in low hiring or promotion rates, pay inequity, or higher rates of attrition for BIPOC employees.

In fact, many of the challenges identified in diversity and inclusion work are actually challenges imposed by structural racism. The most common place I see this dynamic is in hiring. Companies are happy to say that they want to recruit more Black and Brown people. But they don't want to drop their referral programs, their preferences for Ivy League schools, or the requirements that people work in person, in offices located far away from their communities or tribal lands in neighborhoods or cities that are hostile to Black and Brown people. That is perhaps why traditional diversity-and-inclusion approaches so often fail: they focus more on interpersonal actions than structural overhaul and mitigation of biased systemic influences.

INTERSECTIONALITY

Intersectionality refers to the ways in which those holding multiple marginalized identities can experience compounding or entirely unique forms of marginalization.

Law professor Kimberlé Crenshaw coined the term in the late eighties to describe how multiple marginalized identities interact and compound harm, in part because of the legal treatment of Black women. In her landmark paper, "Demarginalizing the Intersection of Race and Sex," Crenshaw analyzed the case of *DeGraffenreid v. General Motors*. During the 1970s recession, General Motors instituted a seniority-based layoff policy, which resulted in layoffs that disproportionately harmed Black women hired after 1964. No Black women had been hired before 1964. The layoffs, Black women argued, compounded previous discrimination. The court argued that it could not create a special protected class just for Black women. The case was dismissed by the court on the grounds that General Motors did hire women—White women—to work in the front office. The plaintiffs were unable to join a race discrimination case by Black men, whose claims did not apply to them. Therefore, because their discrimination did not neatly fit into the boxes of gender or race, they were prevented from receiving justice.

At work, intersectionality can be helpful in understanding the unique experiences of those holding multiple marginalized identities and responding to their needs. For example, in the workplace the primary beneficiaries of affirmative action have been White women. Meanwhile, women of color are paid less, harassed more, and excluded more often than their White female peers. Further, women of color of different races face different challenges. To illustrate, an Asian American woman may not have to prove her competency as often as an African American woman, but she may be penalized more harshly for asserting herself in the workplace. It goes far beyond race and gender; older women, disabled women, trans women, and queer women all face unique marginalization at work. The marginalization can be even more severe where these identities overlap. Supporting all women means understanding the ways that the unique interplay of race, gender, sexuality, class, disability, and immigration status affects their experience at work.

As a Black woman, I think of most of my experiences with marginalization as intersectional experiences. It's hard to tease apart my race and my gender to identify which of these might be motivating bias that comes my way. Even where there is only one differentiating factor between me and someone else—race when I'm experiencing microaggressions from a White woman or gender when I'm being talked over by a Black man—it's hard to know if these experiences are happening because I am Black or a woman or Black and a woman.

Lately, the term "intersectionality," like "unconscious bias," has entered the popular lexicon. And like "unconscious bias," the term has been misused or used in such a way as to undermine antiracist efforts. I commonly hear the word "intersectional" used to refer to any aspect of identity, whether it's inherent or chosen—like hair color, eye color, or clothing style—whether or not those traits are sources of marginalization. Once, at a conference I heard my co-panelist, a blond White woman, refer to blond hair as a source of intersectional identity. This line of reasoning encourages people to conclude that ultimately everyone is impacted by intersectionality. Doing so diverts attention from genuine marginalization, which disproportionately impacts people of certain identities, and toward identity generally, which is something we all have. It renders the term meaningless.

Another common mistake that people make is calling others or themselves "intersectional." In those cases, intersectionality becomes a concept to describe individuals instead of the marginalization they face. The effect is similar. The focus is taken off the marginalization and put on identity, undermining the true meaning of the term.

ANTIRACISM

If you've picked up this book, you might have heard the term "antiracism." You might even be wondering how it's different from just, like, *not being racist*. You might also be wondering if antiracism is something that makes sense to strive for at work and if we really need to lean into it to create more diverse and inclusive organizations.

I have answers to all of those questions!

"Antiracism" is a term that refers to intentional actions

and efforts to actively undo or counter interpersonal, systemic, and other forms of racism.

Though it's often seen as a recent phenomenon, antiracism has deep historical roots in the abolition and emancipation movements. The term was first used in 1943, but little is known about its origination. Since as early as the seventeenth century, resistance movements in the United States and Europe have fought in organized ways against colonialism, slavery, and racism. Scholars like W. E. B. Du Bois and his literary executor, Herbert Aptheker, chronicled the ways in which African Americans and White Americans collectively resisted slavery and other forms of racialized classifications and systems of governance.

Recently, historian and author Ibram X. Kendi, the founding director of American University's Antiracist Research and Policy Center and Boston University's Center for Antiracist Research, popularized the term in his book *How to Be an Antiracist*. In that book he examines antiracism through multiple lenses, including those of policy, biology, culture, gender, and sexuality.

However, that wasn't Kendi's first examination of the term. In his previous book *Stamped from the Beginning:*

A Definitive History of Racist Ideas in America, Kendi frames the fight against racism as a three-sided battle, a battle of complex antiracist ideas warring against two types of racist beliefs at the same time: assimilationist ideas predicated on the notion that there is something inherently wrong with Blackness, and so Black people must assimilate; and segregationist ideas, which blame Black people for their condition in order to justify its continuation.

The concept of antiracism is often situated in contrast to nonracism. Some see reactions to racism as a spectrum, with racist and antiracist on each end and nonracist as the default neutral. Proponents of antiracism believe that so-called neutrality—not actively fighting racism—allows racism to persist, and so is itself racist.

According to Kendi,

> *One endorses either the idea of a racial hierarchy as a racist, or racial equality as an antiracist. One either believes problems are rooted in groups of people, as a racist, or locates the roots of problems in power and policies, as an antiracist. One either allows racial inequities to persevere, as a racist, or confronts racial inequities,*

as an antiracist. There is no in-between safe
space of not racist. The claim of "not racist"
neutrality is a mask for racism.

IS YOUR WORKPLACE RACIST?

The short and simple answer is nearly certainly yes.

The more nuanced answer is still nearly certainly yes. However, if you plan to have a conversation with your boss about racism, especially about the racism you see in your organization, you'll need to point to something much more specific than pithy assertions and feelings.

So how do you know for sure if your workplace is racist? You can't, but there are signs.

Given that racism may be hard to identify and can manifest in a variety of ways, it's not always clear when it's happening at work. As I've said before, in most professional situations there will be an inherent lack of certainty that complicates the work of antiracism. Moreover, all workplaces are impacted in some way by structural racism. But there are certain patterns and outcomes that indicate the presence of racism and require strong intervention. If you see disparate outcomes across race in the following ways, your workplace is probably at least a little bit racist.

THEY KEEP HIRING WHITE PEOPLE

Our workforce is still very much segregated. One of the ways this segregation is maintained is through a failure to hire employees who reflect the diversity of the labor market. Consider, for example, that hiring discrimination across industries hasn't improved for African Americans since 1990. Research has shown that applicants who submit résumés with White sounding names are 50 percent more likely to get called for an interview than résumés with Black sounding names. A 2003 study found that employers were more likely to hire White people who were formerly incarcerated than Black people without a criminal record. After states enacted laws to prevent employers from asking about criminal history, Black men faced worse hiring discrimination because they were preemptively weeded out of the hiring pool by employers who were still racist and assumed that Black men had criminal records.

African Americans are underemployed. They are overrepresented in low-paying jobs and underrepresented in professional jobs, proportionate to their share of the population and their qualifications. Even when controlling for education, duration of unemployment, and cause of unemployment, African Americans consistently are unemployed at twice the rate of White workers.

Though African Americans make up 13 percent of the workforce and Latinx workers make up 17 percent, Black and Latinx employees are dramatically underrepresented proportionate to their presence in the workforce in STEM, the law, arts and entertainment, and architecture. In these fields, representation for each group hovers between 5 and 7 percent. In tech, the industry where many of my client companies are situated, the numbers are even worse. In many large tech companies, only 2 or 3 percent of workers are Black or Latinx.

Hiring discrimination can happen during any of the part of the hiring process—when writing and posting the job description, during résumé screening, during the interview process, in the candidate evaluation process, when determining a salary and title for an employment offer, and while extending the offer.

Structural racism can also impact the hiring process.

Organizations that favor referrals, graduates from certain prestigious schools, or local candidates bring structural racism into their hiring process. Interviewers who emphasize "culture fit" are likely reinforcing structural racism. Structural racism creates and solidifies segregation and poorer outcomes in our social networks and our higher education, housing, and transportation systems.

THE HIGHER UP YOU GO, THE PALER IT GETS

Our workforce is not just segregated by occupation; it is also racially segmented. This phenomenon means that the higher up the organizational ladder you go, the more White employees there are. African American, Latinx, Asian, and Indigenous workers are woefully underrepresented in executive and board-level leadership positions across industries. Since 1999, there have only been eighteen African American CEOs on the Fortune 500 list. Google's leadership is 2.6 percent Black and 3.7 percent Latinx. Fewer than 20 percent of studio executives, showrunners, and producers are non-White. Just 2 percent of law firm partners are Black. Only 10 percent of all board directors identify as persons of color. While Asians from some demographic groups have achieved some visibility at the executive level, they also remain woefully underrepresented. Thanks to the result of cultural stereotypes about Asians that prevent them from being seen as leadership material, White men and women are 154 percent more likely to hold executive roles than Asians.

I call this phenomenon of higher and lighter "the reverse ombré." I see the reverse ombré just as often in organizations that are in the news for breaking down barriers related to diversity as I do in organizations that have very little diversity. It happens not just in sectors where Black and Latino people are underrepresented, like tech, but also in occupations and organizations where they have better representation, like the nonprofit sector.

Fighting racism isn't just about increasing representation, it's also about increasing access to power. Recall that power is a core component of racism. Power systemically solidifies the advantages conferred by racist people and institutions across society. Increasing access is the first step to dismantling this racist system of power and subordination.

POC DON'T GET REWARDED
OR PROMOTED

Disparity in leadership is in part driven by racist bias in performance reviews and promotions. Organizations often struggle in general with assessing and rewarding work. Performance reviews are inherently biased, most employees dislike them, and they have little to no impact on performance. That said, they can be particularly fraught for employees of color. Where there is racism, performance reviews can be used to impede the advancement of people of color or as a tool for retaliation.

The types of bias most influential in the performance review process include:

- Prove it again—the requirement that people from some groups have to prove themselves again and again, in new and different ways, while others don't

- Competency—biased assumptions about who is or isn't competent

- Tightrope—the delicate balance of being seen as too aggressive or too amiable to be taken seriously

- Like me—the preference for those like ourselves
- Performance attribution—where success in dominant groups is attributable to talent or competency and failure is attributed to bad luck, and where success in marginalized groups is attributed to luck and failure is attributed to an inherent lack of talent or skill

When promotion decisions are untransparent and/or unstructured, there's even more room for bias to creep in.

The bias in performance review and evaluation has a detrimental impact on promotion rates for people of color. African American, Latinx, and Asian employees all have higher rates of promotion when their manager is the same race as them. In fact, the promotion rate for African Americans is 79 percent higher when their manager is of the same race. Bias in promotion processes is particularly bad for women of color, who struggle to attain leadership positions. Despite women of color being 18 percent of entry-level employees and expressing the desire to be promoted at higher rates than their White counterparts, only 9 percent of senior director positions,

6 percent of vice presidencies, 5 percent of senior vice presidencies, and 3 percent of C-level positions are occupied by women of color. This drop-off dwarfs those of men of color, who comprise 18 percent of entry-level employees and 12 percent of the C-suite, and White women, who make up 29 percent of entry-level employees and 19 percent of C-level positions.

Where POC actually do make it to manager roles, they are still vulnerable to racism in performance evaluation. While POC managers tend to treat White employees better than White managers, White employees are significantly more likely to express dissatisfaction with a manager who is a person of color than a White manager.

THE WHITE PEOPLE MAKE ALL THE MONEY

Failure to recognize competency or performance disproportionately impacts people of color financially. In organizations where racism is an issue, underleveling and failure to attain pay equity are also likely to be issues.

Typically, conversations around pay equity focus on the uncontrolled salary gap—the salary gap that looks at the median income for each racial group, without accounting for occupation, education, or years of experience. Understanding the uncontrolled salary gap is important to helping us understand structural racism, as it provides us with an indicator of the broad impact of inequality. However, when looking at any given organization, it is also helpful to examine the controlled salary gap, the discrepancy that exists when controlling for the same job and qualifications. Ultimately, it's necessary to look at both to understand the extent of pay inequity in any organization. This information is rarely available to a rank-and-file employee; it can be hard even for those in HR to compile. This lack of transparency and incomplete data collection is itself part of the problem.

If you're curious about how your compensation stacks up, I recommend talking to a White guy. I often ask my White male friends about money and how much of it they receive, and without fail, their answers always blow my mind. If you are a White guy and you are reading this book, you should be open with your non–White guy friends and colleagues about how much money you make. (I mean, don't throw it in their faces, since it's likely to be more. But be open.)

People of color are likely to be paid less than White people for the same role. Additionally, in many organizations, people of color are also underleveled, hired into more junior roles than their similarly qualified White counterparts, and penalized for negotiating their salaries. They are also less likely to be interviewed for some roles than their White colleagues. And, as previously noted, they are more likely to receive unfavorable performance reviews. All of these factors contribute to the salary gap. And when organizations ask for salary history during the hiring process, the impact of the pay gap can follow and compound for persons of color as they move from company to company throughout the duration of their career. It's a sign of progress that this practice is falling out of favor, as many states have moved to ban it.

THE WHITE PEOPLE GET TO DO ALL THE FUN, GLAMOROUS STUFF

Not all assignments are created equal; even coworkers at the same level can have different access to opportunity. When it comes to high-visibility projects, racism can affect who gets considered for the best assignments.

Research has shown that people of color, particularly women of color, are more likely to be asked to do "office housework"—the behind-the-scenes planning and administrative work that keeps things moving—and less likely to be asked to do the highly visible, glamorous work that leads to accolades and promotions.

Tasks related to office housework often include labor that is traditionally feminized and racialized, like fetching documents, taking notes, cleaning up after coworkers, and planning parties. Assignments such as heading a diversity or culture committee, when not tied to internal metrics, additional compensation, or formal job duties, are also considered housework.

Office housework performed by POC typically goes unnoticed. Worse, it's expected from POC employees. These expectations are driven by stereotypes around how POC should behave in the workplace and where they belong in the employment hierarchy. Because feminized and racialized labor is also often undervalued, engaging in these tasks regularly can reinforce a power dynamic that places people of color in lower positions than their White counterparts.

Ultimately, office housework is an impediment to promotion. But employees of color can't just refuse to do it. At a high level, those who engage in behaviors that don't conform to racial stereotypes at work may be ostracized or penalized for not conforming. When it comes to office housework, those who don't volunteer in the face of social pressure or accept the tasks assigned to them may be branded as being uncooperative or not a team player.

WHEN SH*T GOES DOWN, HR IS NOWHERE TO BE FOUND

Ever heard the phrase "HR is not your friend"? It's meant to remind you that in most companies the primary goal of the human resources department is to mitigate risk for the company, not to serve your interests as an individual. When your interests and the interests of the company diverge, most HR professionals will focus on protecting the company.

For people of color inside of organizations, HR can be especially pernicious. The risk-mitigation priorities of many human resources departments incentivize them to minimize allegations of discriminatory conduct, shift the burden of proof of discrimination onto marginalized employees, and sweep serious allegations under the rug. Further, HR employees have their own biases, which may be reinforced by their organizational interest. While several companies have started to create alternative mechanisms to limit HR's role in sexual harassment cases, far less has been done to create alternative channels to report racist harassment or misconduct.

In my experience, the ability of an organization to build a culture of accountability is heavily dependent on the willingness of HR to hold people responsible for their actions. HR departments that fail to hold racists accountable send a message. Employees may be discouraged by the lack of action from reporting cases, and problematic employees may feel emboldened to continue racist behaviors. Organizations with no HR department face the same challenges.

ALL THE PEOPLE WITH MELANIN
KEEP LEAVING

Perhaps the strongest indicator of racism within a company is the rate of attrition for people of color, or the rate at which people of color leave it. Many organizations focus on recruiting a diverse workforce, yet far fewer pay attention to the growth, engagement, and care of their POC employees. Ultimately, failing to create an antiracist organization results in the departure of those who feel targeted, marginalized, and excluded. Employees of color and White employees both quit toxic organizations. Voluntary attrition costs companies substantial time and resources in terms of investment lost, time spent retraining, and hits to their organizational reputation. It is estimated that voluntary attrition due to toxic workplace cultures costs the tech industry alone $16 billion per year. Sometimes, separations that appear voluntary, aren't: Black and Brown employees are also more likely to be forced out of organizations where they have raised concerns about workplace culture or the way they are treated.

Just as telling is the rate at which Black and Brown employees are laid off, fired, restructured, furloughed, or otherwise involuntarily separated from an organization. This can be because of interpersonal or structural racism; for example, African American, Asian, and Latinx employees are less likely to be dismissed when their manager is the same race as them. This is likely due to the presence of in-group bias and the absence of negative interpersonal biases based on race. At the same time, as the General Motors court case mentioned earlier in this chapter shows, seemingly neutral criteria for involuntary separations, such as performance ratings, tenure, division/job assignment, and seniority can disproportionately impact people of color because of structural forces.

Chances are that your workplace struggles with at least some of these issues. If that's the case (which it almost certainly is), then I have bad news and good news. The bad news is yes, your workplace is racist. The good news is, you're not alone, since most American workplaces are racist (back to the bad news!). While you won't be able to fix all of these disparities, you can most likely make things a little bit better for yourself (if you are a POC) or your colleagues of color (if you are an ally). So let's talk about how to get started.

WHO DO YOU THINK YOU ARE?

UNDERSTANDING YOUR IDENTITY, PRIVILEGE, AND POWER

Y ou probably bought this book not just because you wanted to but because a part of you *had* to. Maybe your eyes have recently been opened to dynamics at work that you hadn't noticed before. Maybe there's been yet another racist shooting in the news. Maybe your boss is problematic. Maybe you just can't take the culture anymore. In any case, something has motivated you to have a conversation about race at work. The first step in figuring out how to have this conversation is understanding how you show up to it. How does your identity influence your perceptions and the ways you will be perceived?

I believe it's always best to start with self-reflection—get real with yourself about yourself. How do you understand your own identity and relationship to racism, your position in the organization, your power to make change, and the likelihood that your boss will be receptive to having the conversation that you want to have? Doing this introspective work enables you to approach the conversation strategically and effectively.

WHO AM I, AND WHY DOES IT MATTER?

As you can imagine, I am often called into conversations about race. Some people even pay me to have them. But those conversations are not always effective. Sometimes it's about overall readiness—the person who I'm talking with (who has paid me to talk to them) isn't ready or doesn't want to have this tough conversation, period. And sometimes the question of readiness is more relational: the person who I'm talking to just isn't ready to have that conversation with *me*.

It's not just about what you say and how you say it. It's also about who does the talking. In fact, I have seen clients have a much easier time opening up to my White colleagues or to my Black male colleagues. Some clients gravitate toward some personalities over others; that's natural. But it's also a function of bias: who people allow themselves to see as competent, who they feel comfortable confiding in, and who they will accept criticism from.

I stopped taking this personally a long time ago and learned instead to give strategic consideration to this dynamic.

Like it or not, our identities play a critical role in the conversations that we have about race. We can't bury our heads in the sand about it. If we're going to be successful, we have to confront this reality and develop conscious strategies to avoid our own biases, manage the biases of others we may encounter, and, wherever possible, leverage our position.

UNDERSTANDING YOUR SOCIAL IDENTITY

The term "social identity" refers to the groups or categories that help determine our sense of self, based on our own perceptions or the perceptions of others of our membership. Race, gender, class, country of origin, age, and religion are all part of our social identities. At work, our occupation, seniority level, and team membership could also be considered social identities. Some social identities are immutable. Some can change. Some confer advantage and some disadvantage based on membership.

For example, I am a queer woman in her late thirties, descended from enslaved Africans, from a middle-class background, who is married to a cis White-passing man. This affects the way others interact with me. Sometimes I experience racism, sometimes I experience sexism, sometimes I experience both. Rarely do I experience homophobia, because of my socially acceptable status of being in a heterosexual marriage. Because of my class status, I also experienced (relatively) easier acceptance at school, and work and social access that other African Americans do not.

My identity has also given me access to educational and professional resources that others do not have. For example, because I was born into the middle class, I've lived with less financial precarity than others. Although I had to take on crushing debt, my pathway to college was still easier than it would have been for someone from a less privileged socioeconomic group. As a result, I was also allowed into professional spaces that other Black people weren't. Because of my education and class signifiers, some White people see me as an "acceptable Black person." I've been told more than once that I'm "not like other Black people."

That said, I am still a Black woman, and society treats me as such. I've experienced job discrimination, been called racial slurs, been followed around in stores, and pulled over by the police for no reason. My class position can't buy me out of that. While my social identities afford me some advantage, they disadvantage me as well.

Where social identity systemically confers advantage, such as the ones I just mentioned, we can think of that as privilege. (Yes, Black people can have privilege too.) Usually, I steer clear of that word, "privilege." It's got a ton of baggage, irrationally pisses off some White people, and can derail a conversation. People tend to see privilege as an absolute concept: you either have it or you don't. They react strongly when they feel they are being placed on the wrong end of that binary. But social identity theory shows that privilege is in fact layered and relational.

Though this book focuses on racism, it's important to acknowledge that other aspects of our identity influence our interactions. We bring all of our social identities to the conversations that we have.

Our social identities can influence the content of our discussion. We may miss certain aspects of discrimination because our membership in a social identity group insulates us from seeing it. We may overemphasize one struggle and underrate another because it personally affects members of our group. We may ignore our own biases or miss intersectional marginalization.

Our social identities can also affect how we are heard. Our words and actions may be interpreted a certain way simply because of our social identity and the biases related to it—White dudes, you're in luck (again!), since competency biases and assumptions of neutrality tend to work in your favor. Our social identity may also impact our ability to be seen as credible, knowledgeable, or neutral on the topic of racism. For example, a younger employee may have their concerns about race dismissed because they're a "woke snowflake Zoomer." If we voice concerns as members of an impacted group, we might also find ourselves being dismissed as too sensitive or paranoid. Early on in my career, I got both. Fun!

To avoid these pitfalls, and to uncover ways that we can leverage identity to build connection, introspection is key.

SOCIAL IDENTITY EXERCISE

List all of the social identity groups that you feel a part of. As a reminder, some social identity groups include race, religion, gender presentation, gender identity, sexual orientation, class, age, country of origin, nationality, and physical ability.

Now ask yourself the following questions:

- Which social identities feel the most salient to you at work?

- Which social identities do you think give you an advantage? What kind?

- Which do you think give you a disadvantage? What kind?

- What are some isms (e.g., racism, colorism, sexism, classism) that you may have internalized? What are some potential blind spots that you might have?

- What are the ways in which your identity can influence the conversation?

- Which social identities do you share with your boss? Where do you differ? How might your boss's identity impact the conversation?

- If you were to have this conversation tomorrow, who might your approach leave behind?

- How does this influence the way you prepare for your discussion? How does your social identity affect your point of view?

UNDERSTANDING YOUR SOCIAL LOCATION

While "social identity" refers to the specific social groups that a person belongs to, social location examines where our identities put us in society or a social system, such as our workplace. Social location is what happens when our identities interact with each other and our environment. Simply put, our social location is our "place." It determines which social forces affect us and the ways in which they do. Our social location influences not only the kinds of power and privilege we have access to, but the situations in which we have more or less power and privilege. Social location is important because it helps us understand why different people might experience an organization differently.

Let me give you an example. At ReadySet, we often conduct climate surveys for our clients. These measure how different employees experience the culture of their workplace and the levels of inclusion, belonging, and satisfaction these employees feel as a group. Almost always, the results of these surveys differ by demographic groups. People whose identities confer more privilege at work (usually White, senior, male people) experience organizations more favorably than those whose identities place them differently (like entry-level employees, women or nonbinary workers, and POC). Sure, the environment is the same. But the location is different.

In a workplace context, our social identities can affect the way we are positioned relative to our colleagues. Our social locations impact the ways in which we interpret our workplace environment and relationships, while also affecting the impact our environment and relationships have on us.

Identifying your social location is an important part of the process of introspection. Understanding where you fit in the workplace social system and unpacking the ways in which your location affects your perception is vital to developing an effective communication strategy.

SOCIAL LOCATION EXERCISE

First, think about your social location. How are you situated in your organization's social structure? Then answer the following questions.

- How does my social location impact my visibility and my ability to be heard?

- How does my social location impact my communication style?

- How does my social location impact my sphere of influence and perceptions of my expertise?

- Given my social location, how do I decenter myself and amplify the voices of more marginalized colleagues?

- What is the social context in which this conversation will occur? How can I recognize and leverage that context?

- How does this impact the way I tailor my message?

WHAT POWER DO I HAVE?

To effectively leverage your social position in order to push for change, it is critical that you understand where your power to influence others lies.

You may not realize it, but you have plenty of sources of power at work. Power can be a tricky dynamic in the workplace. We know it exists, but often it is really hard to pin down how that power works and how we can make it work for us. For those of us on the margins, who lack seniority or come from underrepresented groups, the way power functions at work can seem even more opaque, and grasping its unwritten rules nearly impossible.

This section is intended to help you break the code. By understanding the way that power typically functions in the workplace and the types of power that you may possess, you can put yourself in a better position to leverage your influence and push for the change that needs to happen.

Our access to power at work has very real implications for career advancement, financial well-being, and class position. Access to power at work can also affect our physical and psychological well-being. A growing body of research links the inability to control tasks, resources, or decision making with mental and physical health problems.

Perhaps even more importantly, knowing the sources of power enables you to demystify the system for your more marginalized colleagues. Racism is reinforced when privileged colleagues hoard power from marginalized colleagues; it is in the best interest of those wishing to maintain power to obfuscate how it's made. To dismantle racism and increase access to power, we must break down these barriers with radical transparency.

As we explore different ways of thinking about power in the workplace, I encourage you to consider the different types of power that you possess related to your social identity, your organization, and your interpersonal relationships. Each may be a source of influence or disadvantage in your advocacy.

UNDERSTANDING SOCIAL POWER

In my work I often encounter Black and Brown employees (and well-intentioned allies) who think they have no power and senior leaders who take it for granted that they have all of the power. In reality, often the distribution of power is much more nuanced, manifesting formally and informally in myriad ways. Not all aspects of power are permanent. Where formal workplace hierarchies might feel more fixed, power is fluid. It can be given and it can be taken away.

There are many definitions for and models of social power—so many, in fact, I could write a book on that alone. But that's not this book. This book is about racism. So instead of trying to give you one objectively true way of thinking about power, I'll share the model that has worked for me. Hopefully, it will also be useful for you.

In 1959, social psychologists John French and Bertram Raven developed a theory to explain the bases of social power. What I find useful about their approach is that French and Raven examined how power enables social influence, and how that influence creates psychological change. Basically, they sought to explain the ways in which one person can use their power to change another person's mind—convenient, since that's kind of what we're trying to do here.

French and Raven proposed six bases for social power: reward, coercion, legitimate, referent, expert, and informational.

Reward: Think of this as the carrot in the carrot-and-stick approach. Rewards can include bonuses, promotions, or preferential treatment. The bigger the reward and the more likely you are to deliver it, the stronger your power. The use of reward power can help strengthen a relationship.

Historically, people rarely got rewarded for not being racist. Lately, however, corporations have started to see a benefit to vocally supporting antiracist causes. In 2018, Nike's sales jumped 10 percent in the quarter in which it released its controversial Colin Kaepernick ad. Racial justice is trending, and it's profitable. Today, companies no longer fear coming out with a Black Lives Matter statement. Taking a stance against racism is rewarded with attention and money.

For employees at many of these companies, the rewards of speaking up about internal culture are less clear.

Research shows women and non-White leaders are often penalized for advocating for diversity at work. White men avoid censure for such advocacy, but they don't benefit from it. While public social support of justice movements makes money, there still seems to be a concern that rewarding employees for similar behavior may cause distraction or friction. That said, recent initiatives such as those tying executive compensation to improving diversity outcomes indicate that attitudes may be changing when it comes to leveraging reward power inside organizations.

Coercion: If reward power uses the carrot, then coercive power leverages the stick. Coercive power stems from the expectation of punishment if change does not occur. Coercive power can have a negative impact on relationships and result in estrangement over time. At work, coercive power could take the form of negative performance reviews, social shunning, or the threat of being fired.

In the societal context, there are plenty of examples of coercive power being used to address racism. Legal prohibitions and lawsuits are an example of coercive power. More recently, boycotts and, in the age of the internet, social media backlash have emerged as effective forms of punishment against individuals, corporate entities, and government actors who engage in racism.

In the workplace, the threat of dismissal or punishment is also sometimes used to discourage racist behavior. However, as recent justice campaigns like the #MeToo movement have shown us, these coercive mechanisms are not always leveraged or consistently applied. Sometimes they are used to discourage speaking out, through threat of retaliation or termination.

Legitimate: Legitimate power is probably the source of power that you are most familiar with. It comes from internalized values that say a person should have power over us. Legitimate power can come from cultural values that privilege folks of a certain race, gender, age, or social class over others. It can also come from formal social structures, like the role of CEO at a company, or can be designated by a legitimizing body, such as during an election. It can be formally conferred or happen as a result of unwritten societal rules.

Just as with other forms of power, it's important to remember that legitimate power can be given and it can be taken away. In some organizations, a person can seem as though they have legitimate power—like a chief DEI officer—but that person may not be given access to the legitimizing mechanisms necessary to exercise it, like a budget, a team with a substantial headcount, or the power to fire someone.

Societally, White supremacy is a form of legitimate power. In our culturally embedded racial hierarchy, White people tend to have more power and privilege than people of color. White supremacy is solidified through social structures like our education system, which maintains White privilege by providing better outcomes for White people than for people of color. These structural forces and cultural norms are further bolstered by the power of legitimizing organizations and individuals who hire, elect, recruit, or promote White people over people of color.

In organizations, racist hierarchies are reinforced by the delegation of legitimate power. Organizations that disproportionately promote and are led predominately by members of a certain racial group confer and reinforce racist legitimate power.

In the conversation that you have with your manager, your manager is likely to have the legitimate power in the relationship. You may also be tempted to look up the ladder for other levers of legitimate power. Understanding legitimate power, its limitations, and where it can be undermined will be helpful to you as you identify allies and work to get buy-in from leadership.

Referent: If you've paid attention to the rise of influencer culture or uttered the phrase "wrong side of history," you probably have a good idea of the mechanics of referent power. Referent power is reputational, driven by respect, admiration, and the desire to be like someone. It can also come from the relationships that a certain person has or groups they may be a part of. Referent power, like many forms of popularity, can be fleeting.

Referent power, or the fear of losing it, can be a powerful incentive to tackling racism. During the Cold War and African decolonization, the US civil rights movement leveraged the threat of the loss of America's moral standing to fight segregation. In fact, many think it was the desire to win allies in the Cold War and not the desire to address inequality that was the deciding factor in *Brown v. Board of Education*.

Internally, referent power can also be an effective tool for addressing racial harm in the workplace. In my work I often see it effectively used by popular, respected, or highly visible employees who leverage their platforms to shine light on issues related to racial justice. I also see the threat of losing referent power as a useful tool in situations where employees use collective power to take a stand, have to work across hierarchy, or are pushing against legitimate power for change. Access to referent power doesn't necessarily depend on one's place in the formal hierarchy. I've worked in low-trust, low-respect environments where the higher-ups have very little referent power and lower-level employees with strong reputations or sizable social media followings have tons of it.

That said, one of the critiques of referent power is that it is empty. For example, critics of hashtag activism focus their criticism on the fear that those who leverage it do so to achieve more referent power without achieving racial justice. And where, for example, companies publish statements for clout without doing any internal work or, worse yet, while still harming Black and Brown communities, that analysis rings true.

Expert: If meritocracy was real, it would be a manifestation of expert power. "Expert power" refers to power derived from experience, knowledge, or special skills or talents. These abilities do not have to actually exist to confer power; the mere belief in them will suffice. In the workplace context, expert power might look like accepting legal advice from an attorney or hiring a specialized person to lead a project.

Expert power can be beneficial or harmful. In positive circumstances it puts knowledgeable people in appropriate positions of influence. However, people can overestimate expert power, privileging specific domain expertise over other important attributes for leadership, like emotional intelligence or strong ethical grounding. In my work in the tech sector, I see a lot of the downsides of expert power. We've all seen the ways the tech sector has developed an almost myopic view of its role in society, in part because of its overreliance on expert power and its dismissal of other viewpoints.

I personally have a complicated relationship to expert power. I believe that when it comes to racial justice, historically, approaches grounded in expertise have been ignored in favor of those that feel good. This emphasis on intuition over expertise has negatively impacted the personal well-being and professional experiences of many marginalized people, who suffer when the comfort of dominant groups is prioritized over what works. But I am also cognizant of the bias inherent in the concept of expertise. More often than not, expertise looks White and has a fancy degree.

Perhaps the most robust way to conceptualize expertise in the context of racial justice is not only through an academic or professional lens but also through the lens of lived experience.

In the context of organizational work, I believe that expert power is best leveraged when we honor the engaged and center the impacted. As you work toward being an effective ally and advocate, I would encourage you to remember that learning is part of the journey. In organizations that value it, offering expertise (whether it is data obtained through careful study or leveraging a lifetime of experience) can confer further legitimacy on your arguments and position you well to push for change.

Informational: Informational power comes from access to or control over information that others may need. In this modern information age, informational power has become increasingly important, as more information becomes available and our society becomes increasingly reliant on it. At work, informational power can look like access to a strategy or product road map, knowledge about promotion or layoff criteria, or confidential information. One need look no further than the proliferation of the nondisclosure agreement to see how important informational power is.

Companies have come to value their own privacy just as much as they value access to information. Where such privacy protects them from external scrutiny or legal liability, the desire to maintain it is even stronger. Think about #MeToo. Much of the power of that movement came from victims coming forward with their own stories and whistle-blowers who outed companies as bad actors. Once the public had access to that information, it became impossible for organizations to deny that harassment was a pervasive problem and more difficult for them to escape accountability.

When it comes to racial equity work inside an organization, information is power too. Knowing your company's hiring stats, its employee demographic breakdown, or the frequency of certain complaints can help bolster your case. Fear of disclosure can also be a motivating factor. That doesn't mean you should walk into a constructive conversation threatening to publicly blast your company; you'd probably get fired. But acknowledging that unfavorable information about your company is a liability can motivate a decision maker to action.

In all likelihood, you have access to multiple sources of social power. Power is not binary; it's multifaceted and fluid. So the question isn't if, it's how—meaning, no matter where you are in an organizational hierarchy, you should move beyond thinking about *if* you have the power to enact change, toward identifying the sources of power you do have and *how* best to enhance and leverage them.

SOCIAL POWER EXERCISE

After familiarizing yourself with the different forms of social power that you may have access to, consider the following questions.

- How have you used each of these forms of power at work in the past?

- Which approach was most effective? Why? Which was detrimental? Why?

- When did you leverage power outside the traditional boundaries of hierarchy?

- What type of power could you leverage in conversation with your boss?

- Think about your boss's power. What type of power do they hold in the organization? What types of power could your boss leverage in your relationship?

- How can your boss's power be helpful or harmful to your cause?

- Think of third parties outside of your relationship to your boss (like your boss's boss or an influential peer of your boss)—how can you leverage their power in your approach?

Take your time with these self-reflections and don't be afraid to revisit them even after your conversation with your boss is over. Antiracism is a practice rooted in continuous self-education, commitment to pushing boundaries, and the ability to radically reimagine what is possible.

That work starts here, with you.

3

STRENGTH IN NUMBERS

LEVERAGING YOUR COLLECTIVE POWER

n 2015, when I started ReadySet, the conversation about bias at work began and ended with unconscious bias. Many in my field were focused on solving problems of racism and sexism at work through individual action. It's a tempting strategy. Individual-oriented solutions make people feel as though they can do something, and make bias in the workplace seem like an easy problem to solve as long as all the good people align their behavior with their values.

I'm a curmudgeon, so of course I disagreed. I'm also

a recovering lawyer, so I insisted on talking about "the system." When it comes to race, I argued, you could fix all of the biased people in your company and still see biased outcomes, because the crux of the problem isn't just individual—it's systemic.

Whenever I beat this drum on a panel or during a speaking engagement, without fail some rightfully overwhelmed person would raise their hand and ask, "What can I do alone to change these systems at work? I'm not a manager and I don't have any power. How can I change things alone?" And it took me a while to figure out the answer to that question. Even though it's written plain as day in the history books, and every social movement from labor to suffrage to civil rights tells us the same answer, shamefully, it took me a few years to come back with the obvious.

You don't.

There are no heroes in this work. People who go it alone get burned out or singled out for retaliation. They often don't have the information, influence, or access they need to shift people away from the status quo.

It takes a lot more than one person to change a

system—whether that be their school system, the voting system, or the system in their workplace.

I hope the last chapter made you realize that you, as an individual, have more power than you think. But you amplify that power when you band together with like-minded people.

We forget about the power of collective action as a method for change for many reasons. Union membership in the United States has declined dramatically since the postwar period. In 1953, about 35 percent of private-sector workers belonged to a union. By 2015, private-sector union membership had dropped to 6.7 percent. When we look at the public and private sectors together, only about one in ten workers belongs to a union. Collective action also suffers from classist beliefs about who "needs" to unionize; union membership is seen as reserved for tradesmen and blue-collar workers. Over the years we've successfully convinced many workers that individual achievement and struggle is the only way to break through workplace barriers.

However, when it comes to improving working conditions, history teaches us that there is strength in numbers. Widespread improvement in conditions at work didn't come from individual actions. It was the result of collective action. Collective power is why Americans no longer send kids to work in factories, why we have fire exits in manufacturing facilities, and why we pay people when they work overtime.

The labor movement and the fight for civil rights in America have always been intertwined. In the first strike on what is now American soil, Polish artisans in Jamestown stopped working until they were granted the same voting rights as English workers. Though African Americans have not always been welcomed in labor unions, Black and integrated unions played a significant role in the twentieth-century civil rights movement. A. Philip Randolph, the founder of the Brotherhood of Sleeping Car Porters, one of the most influential majority-Black unions, organized the March on Washington movement in 1941, and Edgar D. Nixon, a member of the Alabama branch of the Brotherhood of Sleeping Car Porters, helped organize the Montgomery bus boycotts in 1955. Labor unions, including the AFL-CIO, the largest federation of unions in the United States, funded the Southern Christian Leadership Conference, led by Dr. Martin Luther

King Jr., and voter registration efforts in the South. In fact, Dr. King's last acts focused on worker organizing; he was killed in Memphis while supporting the sanitation workers' strike there.

Today, worker organization doesn't just look like unionization. Organizations like the Fight for $15, whose lobbying efforts have indirectly and directly increased wages for nearly 22 million workers nationwide, and the Coalition of Immokalee Workers, who improved working conditions and wages for Florida tomato pickers, show us that there are many ways that collective action can result in positive changes in the workplace and society at large. Campaigns like the 2018 Google walkout over workplace sexual harassment demonstrate that collective action can result in change at the company level. Actions like the "Shitty Men in Media" list show that they can happen across an industry.

In 2020, in the midst of a violent campaign of police killings of unarmed Black people and the social movements that have erupted in response, this modern labor consciousness has turned its attention to the fight against racism. In an unprecedented move, during the middle of playoffs, NBA players struck. Their forty-eight-hour work stoppage resulted in the creation of a social justice coalition and an agreement to turn arenas into polling places for the 2020 election.

Organizing doesn't just happen organically. Whether we're talking about highly structured unions or rapid-response worker campaigns, these initiatives require careful organizing and planning, especially to identify allies and attract supporters. The same will apply to you as you gear up to tackle the topic of race in your organization. After all, you are preparing for more than just one conversation—you are getting ready to change a system.

HOW DO I IDENTIFY AND ENGAGE COWORKERS WHO MIGHT BE HELPFUL?

For some of you, this may seem obvious. If so, feel free to skip ahead. But for those of you who aren't sure where to start when it comes to building relationships at work, tactical or otherwise, please read on.

The first step (and probably the easiest) in engaging others is to identify the people who are already into (or doing) what you're into. Admittedly this is a lot easier if your organization is one that is open to diversity and inclusion, social activism, or worker-led initiatives. However, even if your organization is more hostile, the first step is the same: find your friends.

This work of fighting racism and the broader political work of changing minds in an organization is all about making friends. Working collectively requires that you find those who are passionate about what you're passionate about, awaken passion in others, then collectively leverage it to make the changes that you want to see. Addressing racism and bearing its effects can take an emotional toll. Having a network of buddies at work can also give you emotional support.

Like some of you, I turned thirty and promptly forgot how to make friends. At work, where organizational hierarchies, competing priorities, and office politics can get in the way, it can be a lot easier said than done. Even so, the typical advice on how to make friends holds true, whether in physical or virtual office environments: be nice to people, engage in small talk, eat lunch with others, join an interest group (like a book club), or hop onto an online hangout. Engage those people in important conversations. See who shares your values and who would be interested in collaborating.

In addition to friends, you'll also want to find and cultivate allies. There's a difference: you have a broader social bond with friends, but an alliance focuses on the achievement of a more narrow shared objective. Workplace allies will be who you rely on to back you up, amplify and spread your ideas, champion your work, provide you with assistance, share vital information, and offer protection if needed. When it comes to addressing racism, forming strong relationships with workplace allies will be critical in maximizing the likelihood of creating impactful change.

When identifying potential allies, look for people who have a demonstrated interest in and track record of engaging on cultural issues at work. Folks who have experience starting grassroots initiatives, like DEI committees, employee pledges, or employee resource groups (ERGs), may also be helpful. Those in leadership or otherwise influential positions who may be sympathetic to your cause, share your values, mentor you, or have a mandate to improve DEI could be useful for your cause as well.

If you work at an organization that already has diversity and inclusion, cultural, or social impact initiatives in place, chances are there are already people tackling issues related to race at work. Those initiatives may be undertaken by ERGs, DEI committees, or culture committees. You definitely should reach out to those folks. Learn about the work they're doing and see if there's a way that you can join forces.

It's important that you align with the existing organizational structure for several reasons. First, you can avoid reinventing the wheel; you'll get greater insight into the efforts already underway in this area and the resources at your disposal. You'll also get the chance to learn from the successes or failures of your colleagues. Second, quite often members of the most marginalized groups drive these initiatives. To ignore their work or proceed without engaging them would make you part of the problem. Particularly if you are not a person of color, engaging in conversations about racism without consulting those most affected by it who are already trying to change your company may result in you centering yourself in a conversation that is about their marginalization; doing so further marginalizes them. If you're new to the topic, it's also likely that you've still got some things to learn, and engaging those with the lived experience of marginalization at your company will prevent you from unintentionally causing harm.

If your company is not friendly to diversity and inclusion or employee activism, you'll need to be more careful. Be mindful of when and how you engage other employees on the topic of race. Remember that not everyone will agree with you, and some may see your activism as a threat. Be cautious when using company computers or communications channels to organize.

Because of its tactical nature, establishing a relationship with a potential ally requires a bit more intention than making friends. As with establishing friendships, you'll want to be a decent human being who tries in good faith to authentically interact with others. But you should also:

BE INCLUSIVE. At this point, I hope that you have started to gain a greater understanding of your own biases. Make sure that they don't get in your way when you try to build relationships. Remember to be inclusive of departments, racial groups, genders, seniority, and tenure.

Don't unintentionally replicate the problem that you are trying to solve.

DEMONSTRATE CREDIBILITY. People want to know that those whom they support will deliver, especially when it comes to an arena as fraught as race. The reality is that finding folks willing to self-educate and engage with the topic of race in a constructive way can be difficult. You don't need to be a know-it-all when it comes to discussing racism or your organization's culture, but you can share your learning, engage in ongoing reflection, and demonstrate a willingness to learn more as you connect with others.

BE RELIABLE. The work of changing the culture of an organization is a long-term project that requires sustainable engagement. Clearly set expectations with your colleagues and consistently fulfill your obligations. Show that you are trustworthy and dependable.

LISTEN. Check in on your colleagues, ask about their unique challenges and broader organizational woes, and actively listen when they respond. Reflect their concerns back to them to show that you've heard and validate their perspectives.

OFFER TO HELP. Move beyond emotional support to action. Do what you can to help potential allies address their challenges or accomplish their goals. If you're not sure how to help, ask.

WHAT ABOUT EVERYONE ELSE?

Most people think of support on questions of social change as existing in a binary: folks are either for an idea or against it. Those who are for your cause are your allies; those who are against your cause are your opposition.

But the real world doesn't work that way.

Typically, support exists on a spectrum. Sure, there are those who will actively support your cause and those who will actively oppose it, but there are also many people who fall in between. You maximize your chances of success if you are able to mobilize those masses and push them closer to your cause.

During the civil rights movement, nonviolent activists saw this spectrum and sought to leverage it in their strategy. Instead of focusing on the already converted and their staunch opposition, they looked at those in the middle—passive allies, neutral parties, passive opposition—and tried to move them closer to their cause. They successfully deployed this strategy during the Mississippi Freedom Summer campaign in 1964. That year, the Student Nonviolent Coordinating Committee (SNCC), a group of young Black college students who led nonviolent direct-action campaigns in the segregated South, realized they needed to turn White people in the North into active allies. The SNCC energized support in the North by engaging White students in a voter registration push in the South, a campaign that became known as the Freedom Summer. More than seven hundred White students joined African Americans in the South to fight against disenfranchisement of Black voters. Those students were radicalized as they saw lynchings, White mobs, and police brutality directed at African Americans trying to exercise their right to vote and at those who supported them. They returned to school in the fall as active allies and organized their campuses.

Those students also wrote to their families, who realized suddenly that they had a personal stake in the struggle. That realization, along with hearing the horrors that their loved ones recounted, converted many northern families from neutral observers to passive allies. Those families then converted their friends and neighbors. This ripple effect drastically changed the political landscape. Later that same year, Congress passed and Lyndon B. Johnson signed the Civil Rights Act of 1964. The following year, the Voting Rights Act passed.

There is power in reaching the majority in the middle. Rather than solely relying on converting their opponents in the South or engaging already sympathetic White students, the SNCC sought to move the larger group of neutral and passively interested people to a place of active interest. In doing so, they created more supporters and were then able to leverage the strength of their collective to push for broader, deeper change.

You can use the same approach at work.

Once you've engaged allies who actively support your cause, think about other interest groups and individuals at work and how much they support your cause, if at all. In crafting your engagement strategy, you must account for not only your allies but also your opposition and everyone in between. Your boss fits into this spectrum too. You are having this conversation to engage them as an ally or bring them closer to your cause.

As you prepare for a conversation with your boss, think about where they fit on what activist, sociologist, and trainer for the Mississippi Freedom Summer movement George Lakey calls the "spectrum of allies." This exercise is a great tool to identify your constituencies, situate them on the spectrum, and brainstorm strategies to move them closer to your position.

The categories along the spectrum are:

ACTIVE ALLIES: People or groups who agree with you and are working actively for the same changes you are. Think ERGs, DEI leads, and employees with grassroots projects.

PASSIVE ALLIES: People or groups who agree with your position but haven't taken action. For some reason, they may not be willing or able to get involved. At work, a passive ally might be a close work friend or someone who expresses interest in culture conversations and who you know is theoretically supportive, but who doesn't actively participate.

NEUTRAL: People or groups who aren't engaged, aren't interested, or aren't informed. They may not have the time or bandwidth to participate in the conversation. There are probably quite a few people at your office who fall under this category.

PASSIVE OPPOSITION: People or groups who disagree with you but aren't actively trying to stop you. They may have interests that compete with yours, or you may make them uncomfortable. These are the people who talk a lot about "meritocracy" or "keeping politics out of the workplace" or "not wanting to lower the bar."

ACTIVE OPPOSITION: People or groups who actively oppose you and are organizing against you. They're the ones who will expend time, money, and resources to make sure you don't get what you want. Think James Damore (the Google memo guy) or the HR lead who's interested only in protecting the company.

The immediate goal is not to move a group or an individual all the way to your side, just to move them one degree closer. You're aiming to have passive allies become active allies, neutral observers become passive allies, passive opponents become neutral, and active opponents become passive.

Fill in each section of this diagram with the individuals or groups at your office that fall under each category. Be as specific as possible.

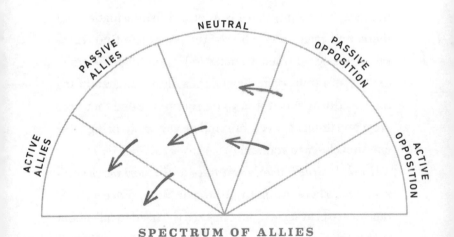

SPECTRUM OF ALLIES

Then think about what you can do to create relationships with those on the spectrum and move them one degree toward your cause. How can you empower passive allies? How can you inform and excite those who are neutral? How can you further disarm or positively engage those who may be passively opposed?

It's really hard to get someone who doesn't care about racism to care about racism, and in today's information-saturated environments, I'd be really skeptical of anyone who has the (socioeconomic, linguistic, and able-bodied) privilege of unfettered access to information pleading ignorance. That said, there is a lot of misinformation out there, and even those who see the issues can find themselves paralyzed when it comes to responding. The effectiveness of any message depends heavily on understanding the context in which it is to be communicated, but here are a few things to keep in mind as you try to bring folks one step closer to your side.

Link external social dynamics to the workplace environment. There are many who can see and accept that racism exists in society but don't see the need to talk about it at work. They might argue that racism is a "political" subject or a topic that has little bearing on the strategic priorities of business. But of course it does; those impacted by racism can hardly leave their identities (and burdens) at the door. Depending on where you work, ignoring racism might actually put your employees in harm's way. Just ask any delivery driver who's gotten the cops called on them for being in the wrong neighborhood at the wrong time, a service worker who has had to deal with a racist and hostile customer, or even a doctor who's been asked to care for a racist patient. Beyond your company's employees, racism likely affects your customers and your product. As you craft your messaging, think about the ways that racism affects your coworkers and your business. Change the conversation from *if* they should get involved to *how*.

Make it personal. Recall our discussion on the power of social identity groups and the roles group membership plays in our social location, messaging, and sense of connection. Leverage that. Make tribalism work for you—emphasize shared group memberships. Articulate the ways in which racism poses a threat to the in-group that you all belong to, whether it's financial, reputational, or moral. Situate your "good" company that stands for something against all those other "bad" ones whose apathy damages the reputation of your entire industry. Give the person or group that you are trying to reach a stake in this fight and get them to see that it is in their own personal interest to join you. Remember, you don't have to be a person of color to be harmed by racism. Just witnessing it can be harmful, discouraging, and traumatizing. Moreover, workplaces that tolerate racism likely also tolerate other harmful behaviors that negatively impact the culture for everyone.

Start with something easy and tangible for them to do. Look, addressing racism isn't like launching a new product or rolling out an engagement survey. Racism is a deeply entrenched social, political, and economic issue that has persisted for literal centuries. It's a lot. And it can seem like a daunting task to take on when you want to get involved. It's also really easy to get discouraged. Help people start small: give them discrete, manageable things to do at which they can succeed. Not everyone has to lead an employee resource group. Tiny actions that get people engaged and make them proud to be engaged move the needle too.

Recognize and reward people when they do show up.

There are some folks who say, "You shouldn't expect a cookie for being an ally. It's just basic human decency." (Me. I am "some folks.") But it is also true that positive reinforcement works. So as you think about your messaging strategy, consider the ways in which you want to recognize and reward those who do show interest. Because there are some workplaces that formally or informally penalize those who do engage in antiracism, creating counterincentives can motivate those who otherwise might sit on the sidelines. No need to make it complicated—positive reinforcement can be as simple as a shout-out on Slack or a private message to say, "Thank you; I see you."

Call people in before calling them out. I can't tell you how many employees and business leaders who I've talked to in my work say that they are afraid to do something to address racism because they're afraid they might do the wrong thing. Sometimes this is horseshit. They just want to blame cancel culture to avoid actually having to do anything. But other times this fear is real. And (I hate to say it) rooted in very valid perceptions of a rush to demonize those who don't get it right. I believe that it is important to have social consequences for problematic behavior, particularly where there aren't other effective mechanisms for accountability. But I also believe we shouldn't rush to punish those who make mistakes. Antiracism is a practice that requires continuous learning. No one, myself included, is done with that learning. People are going to make mistakes. When—not if—they do, and if they are open to learning (this is the real question), it makes more sense to educate them and model compassion than to rush to condemnation. Shaming alienates not only the person who you're trying to engage now but also those who might want to engage in the future.

NOW THAT I'VE GOT ALL THESE ALLIES, WHAT NEXT?

Your relational work doesn't stop with gathering your allies. Now that you've mapped your relationships, it's time to map the relationships of the person that you want to reach. Specifically, it's important to understand who can influence your boss and engage them.

Influence can manifest in a lot of different ways. Recall our chapter on power. Think about which internal and external individuals and organizations might have power over your boss—legitimate power, referent power, expert power, etc. Who does your boss answer to? Who do they admire? Whose opinion do they respect? Who are they most likely to listen to? In political contexts like

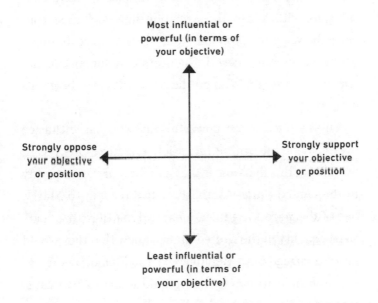

the workplace, especially when it comes to charged topics like racism, sometimes the messenger is just as important as the message.

Just as you mapped your allies, you can also map these influencers.

Place each of the organizations or individuals that you've identified on the chart on the previous page. Then think about who you and your allies already have relationships with. Where those relationships don't exist, consider the ways that you and your allies can create them. Think about how these influencers can support or deliver your message. Who on the map will have the greatest impact?

Leveraging a more powerful ally who has influence over your target can be incredibly effective. One recent example of this dynamic is the fight for marriage equality in the United States. Activists with Freedom to Marry, one of the largest organizations working to realize marriage equality in the United States, knew that they would have to engage both Republicans and Democrats to secure the right to marry for gay and lesbian Americans. Instead of directly targeting Republican lawmakers, they targeted Republican donors. These powerful individual donors helped them secure the right to marry in New York in 2011. They also created the super PAC American Unity to back Republican politicians who supported marriage equality. That PAC and its associated nonprofit successfully lobbied Republicans to support gay marriage in Rhode Island and Minnesota. These state-level victories paved the way for the Supreme Court to strike down the Defense of Marriage Act, which defined marriage for federal purposes as existing only between a man and a woman, and for the Justice Department to federally recognize marriages permitted at the state level.

As you start this process of identifying allies and influencers and brainstorming ways to engage them, you might find yourself feeling a bit like you're engaging in a political campaign. That's because you are. You may not be shaking hands, kissing babies, or tap-dancing for donations. But you are trying to convince influential people to engage with a thorny issue in the hopes of positively changing your environment. That environment, your workplace—like all workplaces—is a political one, and your success or failure has political implications.

Engaging existing allies and creating new ones is a key component of building the collective power that's so useful when trying to push for large-scale change. There's no reason to go at this alone. While your conversation with your boss may be one-on-one, having the backing of a collective empowers you to approach it from a position of strength and can shift the balance of power in your favor.

4

BEFORE YOU
UTTER A WORD

PREPARING FOR A
DIFFICULT CONVERSATION

t this point, you probably feel super empowered. Enraged by the news and armed with knowledge *and* work friends, you're raring to go, ready to leap into a conversation and move your boss to act. With all the work that you've done, how could they not be convinced?

Hold your horses there, cowperson.

It's important that we deliberately plan for these conversations and listen to those who know more than we do.

Remember that this isn't just about you or what you want. Showing up as an ally means making sure that the actions you take actually benefit the groups that you want to support, not just signal your enthusiasm or that you're a good person. Keep in mind that there are layers of complexity here. Research shows that upward feedback—the feedback that you give your manager—is of mixed effectiveness and can have unpredictable results. Some managers respond to upward feedback by changing their behavior, and some respond by rationalizing it away. Moreover, conversations about race can be fraught, provoking distance and defensiveness in people who are not used to having them. You need to prepare to navigate these dynamics, unpredictable as they are.

I FEEL READY, BUT HOW DO I GET *MORE* READY?

Though it may feel like you have already been on a long journey of preparation, your preparatory work is not yet done. Your conversation may not turn out to be difficult, but you should prepare for it like it will be. Anticipate the stress that you will feel. Conversations about race have been shown to trigger stress responses (heck, even being around other races has been shown to cause stress). When you add in workplace power dynamics, talking to your boss about race is a stress double whammy.

When we're stressed, our bodies release cortisol, a hormone that helps trigger our fight, flight, or freeze responses. It shuts down the prefrontal cortex, the part of our brain that helps with complex cognitive behavior, personality expression, decision making, and social behavior (the very functions that come in handy when we're having a difficult conversation). As a result, we become more reactive, more sensitive, and more likely to focus on the negative. The effects of cortisol on our brains can last for days and return as we reflect on the source of the stress, inhibiting our ability to navigate tricky conversations precisely when we need to most. To combat the effects of cortisol, you have to prepare. Preparation sets you up to make your case smoothly and to respond deftly should you face questions or criticism. You don't want to try to wing it when cortisol is coursing through your veins.

UNDERSTAND WHY THIS IS
IMPORTANT FOR THE BUSINESS

It's important that right off the bat, you are able to clearly articulate why you want to have this conversation and how it's important to the business, without getting emotional in ways that hurt your argument.

In my experience, there are several cases for antiracist action that tend to resonate with organizations: the business case, the ethical case, the risk case, the legal case, and the societal case. As you formulate your argument, think about which case or combination of these cases is most likely to resonate with your boss.

The business case. This is the case everyone leads with, and it's easy to understand why. The business case for racial diversity, equity, and inclusion is sound, straightforward, has been replicated across countries, and directly implicates the bottom line. Scholars have been pushing it since the 1990s. The case is simple: diverse and inclusive organizations perform better over time. Diverse and inclusive organizations are more innovative and make better decisions. They have better sales revenue, market share, and customer relationships. While it's true that increasing diversity within an organization can create friction as those from different backgrounds learn to communicate and collaborate without the shared contexts, language, and culture of communication that homogeneity provides, the long-term benefits to the health of the organization and the well-being of employees far outweigh these costs.

Organizations that aren't diverse and inclusive also face additional challenges, like turnover. Technology has the highest turnover rate of any sector. While multiple reasons contribute, including competition over talent, the limited lifetime of most start-ups, and the volatility of the sector, perceptions of equity play a huge role. Overall, unfairness in the workplace costs US employers $64 billion per year. That's the GDP of a small European country.

However, reliance on the business case for tackling bias and promoting inclusion does have its downsides. The first is that it hasn't worked well so far. The business case for diversity has been around for decades, and racial discrimination in hiring and advancement still persist. Some research has found that making the business case for racial diversity might actually make listeners less inclined to be inclusive, as message recipients may not fully trust the business making those claims or may feel as though such assertions threaten their own performance. Focusing on business outcomes can also divert attention from the fact that individual and societal well-being are good in their own right. And because the business benefits take time to manifest, proponents may feel discouraged or lose interest if the organization fails to perform in accordance with their expectations or faces a crisis (as was the case for many organizations during the onset of COVID-19). Finally, awkward messaging around the business case may lead those from underrepresented groups in an organization to feel tokenized or as if they are a means to an end rather than being embraced for who they are.

The ethical case. Increasingly popular, especially given the rise of the Black Lives Matter movement, is the ethical, or moral, case for addressing race at work. That case states simply that achieving equity at work is important because it's the right thing to do. The moral case resonates with people who may feel deeply troubled by inequality or who recognize the ways in which it touches those whom they care about. Appealing to the moral sensibilities of empathetic White people was instrumental in gaining support for the civil rights movement. Today, as we watch police murder people of color and violently crack down on those who protest police brutality, appeals to morality have again emerged as effective tools for advocacy.

Personally, I witnessed the power of the ethical case for diversity during the social unrest of the summer of 2020. As people took to the streets to protest the murders of George Floyd and Breonna Taylor, organizations were forced to reckon with the racism festering within their ranks. My consulting company, ReadySet, was flooded with calls from leaders begging for help. Clients went from being afraid to say the word "race" to wanting to discuss White supremacy and structural racism. It had always made business sense for them to address these issues, but they were compelled to do so only because they finally felt morally obligated to.

Of course, the moral case isn't a silver bullet. There are leaders who don't want to take a stance and would prefer to "just focus on the business" (as if you could opt out of morality). Others hear the word "moral" and immediately slot diversity, inclusion, and racial justice into the "nice to have" category in their brains. But because the moral case can feel subjective and squishy, even if leaders take it seriously, their approaches to solving the issue can also lack rigor and emphasize what feels good over what the evidence says works.

The risk case. This is an increasingly powerful argument for creating an antiracist culture in the workplace, as social media campaigns have become more effective and consumers and employees have become more invested in aligning with businesses that have a positive social impact. Simply put, the risk-based case says, "When it comes to the potential for scandal or backlash, you can't afford to take that hit."

There are plenty of cautionary tales for you to reference. Snapchat lost $800 million after Rihanna criticized an advertisement that featured her and seemed to promote domestic violence. Starbucks lost around $16 million in sales when it closed its stores for a day to train employees following a series of high-profile racist incidents in its stores. In the past few years, scandals related to racism have forced the resignation or replacement of the CEOs and founders of Papa John's Pizza, CrossFit, Chicago's renowned Second City improv theater, women-only coworking space The Wing, lifestyle website Refinery29, clothing brand Reformation, *Essence* magazine, and Hearst Magazines, among many others. Critique "cancel culture" all you like, but no one wants to become the next Twitter hashtag.

The legal case. Like the risk case, the legal case centers the liability of an organization for tolerating racist behavior or maintaining a racist culture. However, the legal case focuses a bit more narrowly on legal liability under local, state, and federal antidiscrimination laws. The legal case is perhaps the earliest compelling justification for racial inclusion in business. On the employee side, the legal case can be traced back to 1964, when Title VII of the Civil Rights Act outlawed employment discrimination based on race, and subsequently to Executive Order 11246, signed by President Lyndon B. Johnson in 1965, which required federal contractors to take proactive steps to guarantee equal opportunity. On the customer side, Title II of that same 1964 Civil Rights Act prohibited discrimination in public accommodation, including restaurants and places of entertainment. As a result, companies enacted diversity programs and opened their doors to a more diverse array of customers to avoid federal sanctions or costly lawsuits.

Although the enforcement mechanisms of state and federal governments aren't as strong as they used to be due to decades of underfunding, and the burden of legal proof for racial discrimination remains fairly high, lost or settled lawsuits related to racism have cost organizations millions of dollars. In 2000, Coca-Cola agreed to pay $156 million to resolve a lawsuit brought by Black current and former employees, who alleged they were under-promoted and underpaid. Walmart paid $17.5 million for hiring discrimination against African Americans. The financial advisory firm Edward Jones paid $34 million to settle a case by Black advisors who claimed they were discriminated against in the firm's training and account distribution practices. Over the past few years, Dell, Intel, Comcast, and Facebook have all paid out multimillion-dollar settlements in discrimination cases. Even when a company doesn't lose or settle, a discrimination case can be costly. Today, it costs on average $125,000 to defend an employee lawsuit, no matter the outcome.

Legal penalties aren't a panacea. For some companies, a million-dollar settlement is a tiny fraction of what they earn in a year. In other words, it's a small price to pay for the privilege of allocating power where they want to and keeping certain people out. Moreover, many employees don't have the resources, knowledge, or time to pursue a lawsuit. Or they may (rightly) feel that the legal system is biased against them.

Some researchers and advocates push back against the legal case for racial equity and inclusion at work. They argue that compliance-based approaches don't work, and in some ways they are right. While evidence on the effectiveness of the case overall is mixed, we do know that training that focuses on legal compliance tends to backfire. Mandatory, legalistic training creates resentment, which can lead to employees feeling resistance and animosity toward antiracist education and action. Research shows that companies that mandate this kind of training see stagnation or even decline in representation of those from historically marginalized groups. That said, other legalistic approaches, like affirmative action, have had some success. Making the legalistic case is tricky because it can result in overindexing on legalistic approaches that don't work, like complicated policies and zero-tolerance rules, while ignoring those that work, like tracking employee demographic data for the purposes of compliance.

The societal case. The final case you may want to consider is the societal case for racial inclusion. Unlike the ethical case, which posits that even if there was no discernible benefit for those in power, racial inclusion is still the right thing to do, the societal case argues that less racism and more inclusion leads to better outcomes for all of us. Therefore, racial equity isn't just the right thing to do; it's the smart (and a little bit selfish) thing to do.

There are a few permutations of this argument and ways in which it can be made persuasively to those with a conscience. One way to make it is to acknowledge that companies that don't account for racism may make products that harm society—not only the racially marginalized (which should be enough) but everyone.

Take Twitter. As early as 2008, it became apparent that platforms like Twitter were hotbeds of harassment for women of color, particularly Black women. Twitter ignored their complaints for years, likely because there were very few people in the company that shared their background or could empathize with their issues. As time went on, the problem of harassment on the platform has only worsened, taking an immense psychological toll on its users. It's also spilled over into the real world, where women have been doxed, stalked, and harassed, all because they are visible online.

The negative impact of Twitter isn't limited to harassment. The company's exclusionary culture silenced early voices warning that the platform could be manipulated for political gain. In 2015, Leslie Miley, an engineering manager of product safety and security and one of the only African Americans in leadership, noticed that there were a significant number of Russian and Ukrainian inactive, spam, and bot accounts on the platform. When he raised his concerns to leadership, they were dismissed. Leslie attributes this brush-off to the company's bias and its refusal to listen to Black voices. According to Miley, when he told his boss what he had found, "the response was, 'Stay in your lane. That's not your role.'" He soon left the company, turning down a severance package so that he could discuss its diversity problems publicly. It might have been a good idea for leadership to have taken him seriously. Just one year later, in 2016, Russian Twitter bots would influence the outcome of the presidential election.

This phenomenon is not just limited to Twitter. You can find examples of biased technology doing harm in the criminal justice system, in hiring processes, and in lending decisions.

Biases can also negatively affect those organizations whose sole purpose is the improvement of society. Some social impact organizations, nonprofits, and foundations harm the communities they serve because those communities are not reflected in their organization. Consider Oxfam, which an independent committee found to have a racist colonial culture of bullying after it was brought in to investigate the organization's culture when Oxfam was accused of covering up sexual abuse of Haitian earthquake survivors by its staff. Or Médecins Sans Frontières, whose Canadian arm released a fund-raising ad featuring a bunch of crying Black children being treated by White (ostensibly haloed) MSF medics set to the tune of REM's "Everybody Hurts," *after* more than a thousand staff members published an internal statement accusing the organization of institutional racism.

Of course, the harm resulting from these individual actors and the biased systems they reinforce is massive. Underemployment of African Americans has cost the economy up to 40 percent in aggregate productivity and output. On a macro level, racism against African

Americans has cost the US economy $16 trillion in lost opportunities for employment, investment, and economic consumption. That's *trillion* with a "T." And that's also just discrimination against Black people, not accounting for the full cost of racism against all POC. If we were to tackle anti-Black racism today, the US economy would see a $5 trillion boost over the next five years. Again, that's trillion with a "T." Who knows how much racism against other groups costs the US economy? I don't, because for some strange reason (racism), that data is hard to come by.

Even groups that supposedly benefit from racist systems are harmed by them. Racism negatively impacts the psychological well-being of those who must justify a system that unfairly advantages them, teaching them to fear or blame those who don't share those advantages.

This case—the societal harm of racism—is why I do this work. Racism holds us all back, and its harms compound as time goes on.

But you don't have to just pick one case. In my experience, it's usually some combination of these justifications that motivates organizations over the long term. The business case is great to get you started, but as discussed, it typically loses momentum once antiracism work is under-way, as people get tired or fail to see immediate returns. When that happens, returning to the ethical or societal cases is often what keeps people emotionally invested and committed.

DECIDE WHAT YOU WANT OUT OF THE CONVERSATION

Once you've landed on how you'd like to frame your argument, decide what you want out of the conversation with your boss. Identifying what you want is important; race is such a loaded topic that it is easy to get derailed in conversation, or for the conversation to turn toward emotion and character judgments rather than a discussion with a particular goal in mind.

In their book, *Crucial Conversations*, Kerry Patterson, Joseph Grenny, Ron McMillan, and Al Switzler offer a framework for identifying and remaining focused on your goals while in a difficult conversation. They recommend that you ask yourself: "What do I really want for myself? What do I really want for others? What do I really want for this relationship?"

These same questions can apply to a conversation about race at work. What do you need from your boss? How would you like them to affect the culture and practices of your workplace? Ideally, what would be the impact of this conversation on your relationship with your boss? How do these goals fit within the overall goal of changing your workplace for the better? You should also be honest with yourself about what you don't want. You don't need to settle for another empty public statement or be the only one to volunteer your time to do more diversity work.

For example, perhaps you want to have a conversation with your boss because there has been another police murder of a Black person in the news, and no one seems to be talking about it. You feel frustrated by the lack of acknowledgment from your team members, especially your boss. You want your boss to acknowledge the social issue and create a dedicated opportunity for discussion. You may hope that this will create a culture of open conversation about racial injustice for the rest of your colleagues. Maybe, you hope, this conversation will help build a culture of empathy or inspire deeper reflection on your organization's own internal racism. Perhaps you and your boss could grow closer as the result of this conversation, or at least develop a shared understanding about the impact that racism has on you and your colleagues.

Articulating and understanding these needs for yourself can help you if you get derailed. They can ground you if your boss becomes defensive or emotional. They can keep you from responding rashly if the discussion doesn't go as you planned. And they can help you assess success or failure once the conversation is concluded.

KNOW YOUR FACTS

When having conversations with your boss, establishing and maintaining credibility is important. Demonstrating an understanding of the facts at hand and the operational contexts in which they exist can go a long way. Being clear that you understand what is within your boss's power and what is outside of it can also demonstrate maturity. More than managing external perceptions, however, this preparatory work helps strengthen your internal compass. When talking about race, it's incredibly easy to get caught up in discussions about intention or to be gaslit into believing that your perceptions aren't true. That's why you need to know your facts.

Before you walk into the conversation that you plan to have with your boss, take some time to brush up on the basics of your organization's context. Consider how it compares to industry practices, its operational constraints (like limited resources, competing priorities, and strategic timelines), its approach to DEI, and its gaps. Pay special attention to the information that will support your case for DEI. To get you started, look for the answers to the following questions.

- How does antiracism align with your organization's values? How does it align with the strategic objectives of your company? Your team?

- What are other companies in your space doing in this area? Who is addressing racism well? How are they doing that?

- What is the current composition of your organization? Of your team?

- Why is antiracism important to you?

- How have you seen race and racism affect your colleagues at work?

- What could your organization do better?

- How does addressing race and racism benefit your organization? How does it benefit your team?

- What would you like to see your boss do?

- What resources can you recommend?

The goal of thinking through and finding the answers to these questions isn't to show how smart or woke you are. That's just going to alienate your boss and whomever else you're having this conversation with. Instead, you want to show that you've thought through the issue and are prepared to answer any questions your boss may have. If your boss asks you to support your assertions with facts, you want to be ready to do so. In the unfortunate case where your boss fails to see a problem, you may need data, both quantitative and qualitative, to convince them.

CREATE A PRODUCTIVE CONTAINER

At the start of every training I do, I say that there is no such thing as a "safe space," but we can make spaces safer. Before we have a challenging conversation, we need to consider how we're going to talk to each other. That's because engaging in these conversations comes with some element of risk, particularly in the workplace context.

It may seem counterintuitive to need to create a safe space for your boss, but it's necessary in order to have the kind of candid conversation that will lead to change. Conversations about race are one of the few sources of race-based stress for White people. While the risks of having this conversation may seem clear to your boss, the payoff may not be.

Your boss may be worried about saying or doing the wrong thing. They may not want to appear ignorant or as though they lack understanding around issues of race. They may think that you think that they or your company is racist and take offense. They may be afraid of a lawsuit. As we discussed earlier, these perceptions of risk can trigger a fight, flight, or freeze response and inhibit your boss's ability to engage in a productive manner.

Now, let's be clear. I'm not talking about changing the content of your message. Especially when it comes to racism, beating around the bush gets us exactly nowhere. Instead, I'd simply like you to be mindful of the context in which you deliver your message. An unsafe context can shut a conversation down before it starts. So use this conversation as an opportunity to call your boss in rather than calling them out. To establish a safer physical and emotional space, keep the following in mind.

Ask permission. It's never a good idea to just spring a serious conversation on someone, especially at work, and especially if the person you're accosting is your boss. You want to avoid catching your boss off guard or making them feel they've been ambushed. Giving your boss the chance to prepare for the conversation will maximize the likelihood that they'll at least start the discussion with an open mind. Remember to keep the request simple and direct. A quick "Can I set aside some time this week to discuss something with you?" can go a long way. That said, you don't want to tell your boss too much up front. Some folks hear the words "race" and "talk" and "to you" and immediately become defensive. Try not to trigger that fight-or-flight response.

Set aside plenty of time. Typically, managers don't have long periods of free time for a heart-to-heart. But it's important that you don't rush the conversation. Productive conversations about race take time: It may take a while for your boss to open up. You may have to sort through difficult emotions, which will require validation and patience. You may need to ask lots of questions to gain a better understanding of your boss's position. You may need to clarify unfamiliar terms or share new perspectives. It may be difficult for you to come to an agreement on actionable next steps. Adding time pressure can exacerbate the stress of the conversation and increase the likelihood of a negative reaction, so make sure you schedule adequate time for the conversation and that you manage your own expectations for what can be accomplished during this initial discussion.

Reserve a private physical spot or virtual channel. Unless you have to interrupt some seriously egregious behavior in the moment (and even after that happens), it's better to have this conversation in private. The presence of others may make your boss feel they're under attack and provoke defensiveness. Particularly if you are offering feedback on your boss's behavior, your boss might interpret public criticism as insubordination. If you speak to your boss in front of others, they might also feel pressure to act more knowledgeable and less open-minded than they actually are. So choose a private physical or virtual space to encourage the kind of transparent and vulnerable conversation you need to have for progress to happen.

Center yourself. This may be a challenging conversation for your boss, but it will likely be emotional for you too. You might feel intimidated; you'll probably be a bit scared. And you'll be navigating these *big* emotions while having a conversation about a tough, deeply personal, and triggering topic. Taking all of this into account, it's easy to see how these conversations can quickly get derailed or spiral, even when both parties have the best intentions. So whatever your practice—deep breathing, meditation, splashing cold water on your face in the bathroom—do that before you utter a word.

OKAY, NOW IT'S TIME to take all of that self-reflection work and preparation and pair them with some *magic words.*

Just kidding. There are no magic words—just carefully considered ones. Let's talk about those.

5

FINDING THE
RIGHT WORDS
KNOWING WHAT TO SAY

Welcome to the chapter that some of you probably skipped to, what we're really here to discuss: *the conversation.*

We've spent quite a bit of time discussing how we prepare for the conversation and how to set up your environment. Now we're going to talk about the words we actually want to say.

Let it be known that I came to this advice the hard way—meaning that I have learned how to have these conversations through painfully awkward and, at times, traumatic trial and error. The first time I tried to talk to my bosses about race, it did not go well. Now, granted, I'm Black (making it easier to dismiss my concerns) and they were White Frenchmen (with a bad case of denial), but the conversation still went surprisingly poorly.

It was my first job out of law school, with an international consulting firm (an industry not exactly known for its inclusive culture). I went to work for them excited to apply what I had learned and hungry for adventure. It was rocky from the start. A few weeks into my new job, my boss accused me, an Ivy League law grad, of plagiarism—apparently, my writing was too good.

Things came to a head after I had been at the company for a few months. One night, my coworkers and I went out for drinks without our bosses, as young aid workers do, in the restaurant across the street from our office. A few of my colleagues got too comfortable. They started telling me about the problems with Black people—not me, of course, but *other* Blacks. As the night went on, they got more aggressive, and the benevolent toxicity got less benevolent and more toxic. They took great pains to tell me that as a Black person I would never be accepted in France, their home country, and that while I was pretty (for a Black woman), that just wasn't enough. It was six on one. No one came to my defense. And I had never felt more let down by an organization that I naively thought had my best interests in mind.

I took a few days to cool down, and then I talked to my bosses. In my heart, I knew what had happened was more than just "drunk talk." I mustered up all of my courage to tell my bosses just that and, again naively, I expected that they would support me. But, of course, I was wrong. Why else would I be telling this anecdote? As a relatively sheltered young person, early in my career, who grew up thinking that I could achieve my way out of White supremacy, I was shocked by their response.

They doubled down and defended my colleagues. They called me overly sensitive. They claimed that what happened wasn't racist. They told me to drop it.

A month or so later, when the time came to renew my contract, they didn't.

I didn't have the language then to fight back. I couldn't articulate why what happened was wrong or why it was important that they take action. I had no idea how to respond when they told me that I had imagined the racism, because I was American and more sensitive (textbook gaslighting), or that they couldn't punish people for what happened outside of the workplace (avoiding account-ability), or that I needed to be a better team player (more gaslighting). All I could do was nod, swallow my tears, and vow to keep my head down—as so many Black people have done before me.

I hope that after reading this chapter, you will walk away better armed than I was. There is no guarantee that by saying the right words you will magically cure a person or an organization of racism. If that was the case, my middle school teacher would have been right, and racism ended with Martin Luther King Jr.'s "I Have a Dream" speech. But having the right words in your arsenal can move the needle a little closer to your side and lay the foundation for transformation.

CONVERSATIONAL TECHNIQUES TO TRY

As we discussed in the previous chapter, most people, particularly those from groups not used to having to talk or think about race, experience some level of fear and defensiveness in discussions about race. For them, these conversations about race can create a type of stress that they are not used to feeling. When setting the stage for a conversation about race, it's important to keep these tendencies in mind and to create a buffer against them. Whether you are looking to start a conversation or advocating for deeper systemic reform, here are some near-universal pieces of advice for structuring this conversation at work, regardless of the reason.

USE A GROWTH MINDSET

Coined by Stanford psychologist Carol Dweck, the term "growth mindset" refers to the belief that talents aren't innate characteristics but rather can be developed through hard work, with feedback from trusted sources and other kinds of support. The same is true of behavioral change. People can change with consistent feedback and accountability.

Racism is the default in our society. We all have racist behaviors and assumptions to unlearn. It's important that we give people the space to grow as we ask them to be better allies. This doesn't absolve them of responsibility when they cause harm, but it does acknowledge that we all need time to learn and make mistakes. Give your boss the grace someone once gave you. Acknowledge out loud that this is a tough conversation to have. Offer to share resources with them. Frame the journey of racial inclusion as one that you are undertaking collectively as an organization. Acknowledge that it is difficult to get things right. Give an example of a personal growth area for you. Highlight areas where your boss, your team, or your organization seem to be doing well.

APPROACH FROM A PLACE OF INQUIRY

Don't assume you know where your boss stands or what might be behind their beliefs. Ask questions. Try to understand their perspective. Don't be afraid to ask for clarification or request that your manager say more about their point of view. Watch their body language and avoid interruptions. Don't forget to use this conversation as an opportunity to learn. Even if you don't get everything you want, you can still leave with a better lay of the land.

Some of my favorite prompts include:

- How is this landing for you?
- Would you mind sharing how you see things?

- What would it be helpful for you to know?

- What should I keep in mind?

- What criteria are you using to determine our approach to this topic?

- How do you see the impact of these conversations?

- Where do you see opportunity?

- What feels challenging?

- Can you say more about that?

CALL IN

Twitter is a great place to call people out. It forces you to be pithy. It lets you slap on a hashtag. When the conditions are right, it helps you start a movement. And, real talk, sometimes it levels the playing field. But your workplace is not Twitter. Treating it as if it is just screws you, your relationships, and your organizational culture in the long run. It can be hard to resist, but just as you did with the potential allies you engaged in chapter 3, try using this conversation with your boss to call in rather than call out.

Calling out relies on shame to change culture. Shame

can be effective at deterring certain behaviors in a larger group, as a tool to establish cultural norms. However, in private conversation and in the context of a hierarchical relationship, shame is a less useful tool. It can provoke your boss to quickly turn defensive or adversarial. You also risk damaging your relationship and being labeled as insubordinate. While it may feel good in the moment to come back with a snappy retort or a catchy phrase, shaming your boss, even unintentionally, can get in the way of your getting what you want from this conversation. Conversely, calling in invites a person to explore their action and impact with you, while encouraging them to view these dynamics from a different perspective.

To be clear, calling in is most appropriate when there is a strong chance that you can reach mutual understanding. If it seems like your boss does have good intentions and you may have some ideological alignment, try calling your boss in before you put them on blast. How do you call someone in?

- Show up vulnerably. Be transparent about why you want to have the conversation and how actions (or inaction) related to race have impacted you. While you should always bring it back to the workplace, drawing from your broader experience can be helpful.

- Ask questions. Demonstrate that you are really interested in where they're coming from. The prompts I listed above are a great start.

- Offer support or resources. When it comes to resources, offer your boss material that is easily digestible, relevant to their position, and from a reputable source. *Harvard Business Review* is typically my go-to for this audience. Feel free to offer a book or two, but curate your suggestions to avoid overwhelming them.

- Share your own journey. What lessons have you learned along the way? If you are White, how did you become interested in antiracism? What spurred you into action? If you are a person of color, how has racism affected you?

- Keep it relational. Emphasize the importance of the relationship you have with your boss and the positive influence they could have in your organization.

PRACTICE ACTIVE LISTENING

What you say is important, but I think that the success or failure of a conversation really hinges on the ability to listen. Listening is how you gather the intelligence that you need to inform your approach. Listening is how we learn—what our bosses' motivations are, the things they may be afraid of, and the narratives they're spinning. So make sure that you aren't just thinking about what words to say next but are truly listening to what your boss is saying and implying in their responses to you.

Further, active listening allows us to demonstrate empathy and build trust. In conversations about race, members of dominant groups often fear being misunderstood. That fear can sour a conversation really quickly. Let your boss know that you hear where they are coming from and can see their perspective (this doesn't mean you have to agree with it).

Throughout the conversation, check in with yourself to make sure that you are actively listening to what's being said. Here are some tips for active listening.

- Maintain eye contact. In all likelihood, your boss is not a jungle cat or an adolescent chimpanzee, which means you should signal your engagement with eye contact. Try the 50/70 rule: make eye contact for 50 percent of the time while you are speaking and 70 percent of the time while you are listening. If you or your boss are uncomfortable with eye contact (perhaps for cultural or cognitive reasons), you don't have to force it. But try to push yourself to make eye contact every now and then—when you're making an important point or asking a question.

- Pay attention to body language—yours and theirs. Lean in toward your boss. Nod your head while listening. Keep an open posture and avoid crossing your arms or otherwise signaling that you are closing yourself off. At the same time, watch your boss and their body language for clues about how they're feeling.

- Occasionally, reflect back what is being said. Use phrases such as "I hear you saying . . ." or "When you say X, do you mean . . ."

- Avoid interruptions or talking over your boss. Resist the temptation to jump in to defend your point or try to complete your boss's sentences.

- Ask follow-up questions. Don't be afraid to ask for clarification. Prompt deeper reflection by keeping questions open-ended.

- Minimize distracting technology: If this meeting is taking place in person, close your laptop. If you are on a video call or in a virtual meeting, close those extra browser windows. And no matter what, put away your phone. Research shows that the mere presence of a phone can be distracting enough to diminish attention and impede performance.

BE DIRECT

Some organizations love euphemisms. "Unconscious bias." "Racial tension." "Politics." "Divisive." "Controversial." "Intolerant." I've heard all of these words used to describe racism and racist behavior without actually having to say "racism." But, as the saying goes, "Words mean things."

People don't like saying the words "racist" and "racism" because it's uncomfortable. These words describe ways of treating people and leveraging systems that we know are morally abhorrent, and remind them of our country's dark history and the villains that lurk within it. All of our lives we've been taught to distance ourselves from that history, to "keep it in the past" where it belongs. After all, the moral arc of the universe is supposed to be bending itself toward justice.

But avoiding uncomfortable words makes us less effective advocates for antiracism. Not calling behavior or systems racist when they are doesn't make them less harmful. And it does lull us into believing that we can respond less urgently. It also inhibits our ability to account for the unique impact that racism has on certain groups of people. For example, if you emphasize "unconscious bias" rather than racism in your conversation with your boss, you are prompting your boss to respond very differently.

An approach to fighting unconscious bias typically involves training to recognize cognitive biases, creating more structured processes to mitigate the influence of personal bias at the systemic level, and auditing for biased outcomes across different races, genders, ages, and ability levels. An antiracist response would focus education on interpersonal and systemic racism; address anti-Blackness; tackle the influence of racism in hiring, promotions, and performance management; create goals for representation and advancement of those from underrepresented minority groups; and crack down on racism internally by enforcing strong penalties for racist behavior.

Further, an unconscious bias response would not acknowledge racism coming from other marginalized groups and could obscure the harm that victims of racism experience within an organization with the success of more privileged minority groups. For example, early diversity initiatives in tech that focused on tackling unconscious bias resulted in improvement in visibility and outcomes for White women in tech, while numbers of Black and Brown workers have stagnated or decreased.

My tips for being more direct? If a racist thing is racist, call it racist. To become more comfortable doing so when the time comes, practice these terms: "race"; "racism"; "racist"; "White supremacy"; "antiracism"; "anti-Indigenous," "anti-Latino," "anti-Asian," and "anti-Black."

Avoid these words: "racially tinged," "racialized," "racially insensitive," "racially motivated." Don't say "people of color" when you mean Black people. Don't say "implicit bias" or "unconscious bias" when you mean "White supremacy" or "racism." Don't talk about "pipelines" if your problem is overt or systemic racism (more on my disillusionment about pipelines in chapter 7). And if the conversation starts to veer toward these "comfortable" phrases and topics, redirect it back to the truth.

FOCUS ON IMPACT RATHER THAN INTENTION

Often in conversations about racism, as we've discussed, the person being approached says something like, "I could never be racist," or "That's not what I meant," or "We mean well." These requests ask us to consider the intention of the persons or systems whom we associate with racism as we point out what needs to change. The thinking here presumably goes that if one doesn't intend racism, then maybe the racism is not so bad? It almost seems like some White people think that being called a racist is actually worse than the racism itself.

This, of course, is not true. Focusing on a White person's intention centers them, their feelings, and their fragility and takes attention away from those impacted by racism and the ways in which they are harmed. It also absolves the White person of responsibility for their actions or for changing the systems from which they unfairly benefit. According to the reasoning of intention, responsibility for change lies with those few terrible people who actually intend to be racist, enjoy the racism, and relish the benefits racist systems provide.

In some ways this makes sense. We have a cognitive bias toward weighing intention when we evaluate harm and accountability for it. We tend to see intent to cause harm as much worse than unintentionally causing harm. Our brains also interpret acts that are intended to be harmful as more harmful than those that aren't, even if the impact of both actions is the same. Which means we have to consciously push against our own instincts in order to hold people accountable for their impact in spite of their intentions.

When White people deny their racist actions because they didn't intend to be racist, it feels like the ultimate form of gaslighting. What does it mean when a White person claims good intentions? It demands that we become certain about what is in someone else's heart before we intervene to mitigate the harm that they may cause—which is impossible. Most people don't possess psychic powers. We could drive ourselves mad trying to

divine what is in someone's heart. And that is the point—
to distract us.

So in order to keep your conversation with your boss
focused on impact, you may want to emphasize the following:

- How race has affected your experience in your
  organization, and how it has affected your colleagues.

- How it has affected your ability to do your job.

- How race or lack of awareness of it has affected
  your relationships with your customers and your
  colleagues

- How it has affected your internal and external
  messaging.

- How it has affected your products and services.

FRAME ANTIRACISM AS A
COLLECTIVE PROJECT

Defensiveness is a common response to conversations
about race because people often interpret feedback on
racist behaviors as an indictment of their character. Some

see any conversation about race as divisive instead of unifying.

We discuss how to handle defensiveness in the next chapter, but you can preempt oppositional dynamics by framing the work of antiracism as a joint project. Instead of "you" statements, use "we." Instead of one-sided demands for change, try framing your asks as part of a collective journey. For example, rather than saying, "You need to do X," try "We all have some work to do. Can we start by doing X?"

APPEAL TO YOUR BOSS'S SELF-INTEREST

Not all people with privilege will engage with antiracism out of a sense of altruism. Consider the theory of interest convergence, developed by law professor Derrick Bell to explain the Supreme Court's landmark ruling in *Brown v. Board of Education,* which we mentioned earlier. Bell argued that civil rights advancements happen not because those in power realize the error of their ways but because they realize that, for whatever reason, it is in their best interest to support the advancement. In the case of *Brown v. Board of Education*, the Supreme Court recognized the need for the United States to maintain a positive image abroad during the Cold War, which segregation undermined.

Frame your case in a way that will resonate with your boss. Seed arguments and feed your boss talking points that could also resonate with your organization's leadership. What are your boss's priorities? Are they concerned with a particular business outcome? Are they afraid of lawsuits? Do they need to hire more people? Do they need to find more customers? Remember the different kinds of cases for antiracism from the previous chapter. Find a way to tangibly link your case for antiracism to these outcomes.

FOCUS ON WHAT YOUR BOSS CAN CONTROL

Just like you, your boss has to answer to somebody. And just like you, they only have so much authority to change things. Make sure that you focus on what is actually in your boss's ability to control. It's a lot easier for your boss to check in with the team after an incident of racial violence happens than it is for them to change the composition of your company's board.

Ask for what you can get. That doesn't mean that you stick to advocating for the small stuff, but it does mean that you should be strategic about your asks. If, for example, you'd like for your company to have more inclusive hiring practices, make sure you understand which parts of the process are within your boss's control. They may not be able to change things overnight, but they could ask for training for hiring managers, standards for writing inclusive job descriptions, support for ERGs advocating for a comprehensive strategic approach, or a meeting with their boss to discuss representation goals.

Set up your boss for success by giving them something they can actually do, and do successfully. A few quick wins can create a positive feedback loop for your boss, incentivizing them to engage on a deeper level for a more prolonged period of time.

KEEP IT ACTIONABLE AND
IDENTIFY NEXT STEPS

Too often, conversations about race get mired in feelings and peter out with vague commitments to "do better." That's where a lot of people feel comfortable. But conversation without action is meaningless. In fact, it may even be harmful, as it asks BIPOC employees to engage in difficult emotional labor without benefit, eroding trust and burning out employees of color and their allies as they try to improve their workplace.

No one is asking you to have all of the answers. It's not your job to fix your company's culture alone. But it would be helpful to have some solutions in mind as you engage in this conversation. If you are approaching this conversation as an ally, make sure that you've consulted those from the most impacted groups and are centering their work as you make these suggestions.

Think of this conversation as a precursor to action, setting the foundation for the steps that you and your boss will have to take to make your workplace less racist. By positioning yourself and your boss to act, you also create a framework for accountability. It's very hard to measure progress against feelings or intention. It is much more straightforward to gauge it against specific commitments to act. So think about some tangible next steps that you and your boss can take that will get you closer to your goal. If you're wondering what specific actions to suggest, check out chapter 8.

Consider the following:

- Where is the low-hanging fruit? What could you do quickly and easily that could be impactful as you work toward long-term solutions?

- What have other companies in your position done?

- What role can your boss play? What are they uniquely positioned to do?

- How can you support your boss in accessing the internal resources that may already be available and building on the work that has already been done?

- Who can your boss loop in that might also be helpful?

- What are you uniquely positioned to do?

There's a chance your boss might commit to action in theory, then shift all of the responsibility to you to actually *act*. Be careful here. It may be tempting in this case for you to go all out—to really push yourself, to work yourself to the bone fighting against forces that may or may not be within your power to change.

Unless that mandate comes with a new title, a raise, and a team, it's a trap.

Whether they realize it or not, your boss is actually setting you up to fail. They are giving you a second job for which you won't be recognized or compensated; you might even be penalized. Chances are you probably won't receive the additional resources or visibility to do it well either. The truth is, if this action was really a priority for your boss, they would find some way to lead it themselves.

If your boss tries to put you in charge, ask them for clear expectations and a written commitment for what this means for your role (Are you expected to work on DEI 20 percent of the time? Thirty percent?). Set boundaries early around what you can and can't do. Ask for resources—a budget and a salary increase. Turn a non-commitment into a commitment.

FOLLOW UP

No matter how it goes, this conversation may be a lot for your boss to process. Recognize that your conversation, like many conversations about race, might be uncomfortable, deeply personal, and even emotional for your boss. Give them a chance to reflect on your feedback and create space for you both to reflect on any lingering feelings that you may have or engage in relationship building that you need to do.

In any case, this conversation isn't meant to be a one-off. Ideally, it kicks off a longer journey through a sustainable process. Follow up regularly to maintain momentum. Doing so will also give you the chance to solidify broad commitments and objectives, nail down responsibilities, check in on next steps, and create habits that reinforce accountability.

During this follow-up conversation, take the same care you did in the first one. Going forward, try making topics like racism, equity, and culture a more regular part of your conversation. Like any other skill, the more you practice engaging on the subject of racial equity, the more comfortable you will be doing it. Normalize it.

WHAT IF MY BOSS IS
THE ONE BEING RACIST?

Oof. I'm sorry. While this is just as likely as any other scenario, that doesn't make it less painful. Maybe your boss can't stop calling all of their Black female employees "girl" in a sassy tone. Maybe they just happen to promote White guys all the time. Maybe they've stayed silent instead of speaking out against social injustice. Sometimes the person most in need of reform is the very person your career progression depends upon.

This is where things can get tricky. Our rational brains tell us that if our boss does or says something racist, maybe we can change their behavior with feedback. However, this approach is risky. Depending on the temperament of your boss, it might not be the best option. If your boss has been resistant to other types of feedback in the past or doesn't seem interested in changing this aspect of their behavior, having this conversation may do more harm than good. In that case, it may make more sense to explore other options, like getting support from your peers, moving to a different team, or talking to HR.

However, if your boss is open to feedback and you think a conversation will influence their behavior, go for it, keeping the following in mind.

Check in with your allies. There are a lot of great ways to stand out at work: take on added responsibilities, successfully execute a project, build your company's social media following. But don't be the only person calling out your boss's racism—that makes you a target. Even if this conversation is only between you and your boss, make sure that you've already engaged your allies so that they can support you if needed.

Ask for consent. If you have observed your boss engaging in racism against someone else, get that person's consent before intervening on their behalf. Even if you don't face any backlash for this discussion, they might become a target, especially if you aren't a member of a marginalized group and they are. The person who you want to act on behalf of may not want you to do anything, because they are more attuned to these dynamics than you. So if this conversation is about a specific incident involving a specific person, check in with that person before you have it. Unless your boss's actions are part of a larger pattern of behavior that also affects you, don't say anything if your coworker asks you not to.

Focus on the action and the impact it had. As we mentioned earlier, you want to avoid veering into any sort of conversation about the character of your boss in conversations about racism that you may have observed. This is even more true when you're talking not about amorphous ideas like culture or the pipeline but the specific actions (or inactions) of your boss. They're probably going to take it personally. So stay focused on the specific action that your boss engaged in. Name it in the conversation. Explain why it was problematic. Describe the impact it had on the team. Propose a way of moving forward.

WHAT IF MY COLLEAGUES ARE THE PROBLEM?

Well, that also sucks. While your teammates don't have the same authority over you that your boss does, their behavior can still significantly impact your experience at work. After all, their conduct is a reflection of your workplace culture, and if their behavior is toxic, chances are there are some other problematic elements at play too. Most of the advice above also applies in this situation. In addition to it, you might also want to keep the following in mind.

Brush up on your organization's rules. Before your conversation with your boss, make sure that you understand the rules that everyone is expected to play by. Review your organization's code of conduct and employee handbook to understand what is prohibited in your workplace and what your protections are. If there has been a violation of some kind, you should be able to name it and be familiar with your resources for responding. Decide whether you want to initiate a formal process or keep this an informal conversation. Consider whether you want to involve HR, if at all. You'll want to avoid surprises if this conversation triggers mandatory reporting.

Keep a record. Document, document, document. Whether or not your boss is on your side, you should keep a record of the racist incidents you observe and the response to those incidents. Take notes. Do so while your memory is fresh and include as many details as possible. What happened in the interaction? Who observed it?

How did you react? How did others react? Who else did you tell? Support those notes with photos or screenshots if you can get them.

Create a paper trail. After your meeting with your boss, follow up by email summarizing the subject discussed and the outcomes. You'll need this documentation should you decide to file a formal complaint or have to defend yourself from backlash.

HR has entered the chat. Likely, by initiating this conversation, you've got your boss thinking about HR, especially if they are risk averse. It almost goes without saying that race is still very much a hot-button issue. Your boss might be worried about being reported or sued. Even if you have no intention of bringing HR into the mix, there will be the temptation for your boss to go into risk-mitigation mode. Depending on your organization's policies and your boss's conduct, mandatory reporting to HR may be required (for example, if you share that another employee on your team has violated antidiscrimination law). Be mindful that this will affect the tone of your conversation and may impact the ways in which your boss is able to respond to your feedback.

. . .

ULTIMATELY, REGARDLESS OF the source of the problem, whichever words you decide to use for this conversation, whatever way you choose to frame your argument, don't forget this most important piece of advice that I am about to give you: *You need to practice.*

Now, will you feel like an idiot practicing eye contact and nodding at yourself in the mirror, or thoughtfully laying out your journey to racial enlightenment to your roommate? Maybe. But you almost will certainly do yourself a disservice if you try to wing it.

In all likelihood, when you have this conversation, your heart will be racing. Your palms may sweat. You may stumble over your words. The cortisol will be flowing through your veins. The only way around the stress response that you will certainly have to manage is through the familiarity and confidence obtained by repetition and refinement.

So practice your arguments. Practice your retorts. Practice your listening face.

Now, there is always the risk that no matter what you say or how you say it, your boss may walk away feeling personally attacked. Sadly, defensiveness is a common reaction in conversations about race. It's quite possible you could take all the care in the world and your boss's response could still be "How dare you call me racist!" I always say we can only control what we can control. Your level of preparation is within your control. The care you take to set this conversation up well is within your control. Your reactions are within your control. Your boss's response isn't.

Good or bad, be prepared for whatever comes your way.

Speaking of which, let's talk a little bit about the bad things that might happen.

6

PUSHING BACK AGAINST THE PUSHBACK

HOW TO HANDLE RESISTANCE

Many of us know the feeling: The sickness in the pit of your stomach. The choice between protecting what you've earned and honoring who you are. We're compelled to have these conversations at work even as we fear that they might backfire. Often, we—especially POC—walk into them cracked wide-open, already hurt, wounds still weeping. We pull it together with the optimistic, maybe naive, idea that maybe, this time, just maybe, we can make a difference. Maybe we can change things.

I've been having these conversations for a while. A list of the things I've lost:

- Friends: Old friends, new friends, people who I discovered never really were my friends. Friends who showed their true colors and friends who didn't show up at all.

- Romantic partners: Those who couldn't see me, or didn't want to, or grew tired the more they did.

- Recognition: For my hard work. For the progress I opened the door to. For the disasters I averted. Of the truth in the things that I said.

- Promotions: Reserved for the ones who fit in, who didn't make trouble.

- Sleep: Wondering if I could have done things differently. Thinking through what it would take to fix myself enough to succeed.

These conversations come at a cost.

When renowned AI ethics researcher Timnit Gebru, one of the few Black women leaders in the field, emailed members of her employee resource group to express frustration around Google's lack of progress with its DEI efforts and the ways that she was being held back, she was fired within days. After speaking out against racism at Cards Against Humanity, Nicolas Carter's employer had him committed to a psychiatric hospital. We all remember what happened after Colin Kaepernick decided to take a knee. For many of us, speaking out against racism carries a risk.

In September 2020, as the Black Lives Matter movement surged back to prominence after George Floyd's killing, and in the midst of a global pandemic that ravaged the US economy, President Donald Trump issued an executive order banning certain diversity trainings. The Executive Order on Combating Race and Sex Stereotyping forbade federal government agencies and federal contractors from conducting training that mentioned "White privilege," "intersectionality," "systemic racism," or "unconscious bias." Separately, his Department of Labor also investigated companies, like Microsoft, that had set internal hiring goals to increase racial diversity. The administration even went so far as to set up a hotline at the Department of Labor for those who wanted to report diversity trainings at their workplace.

The executive order from President Trump, himself

the byproduct of the backlash to the country's first Black president, can be situated in a historical continuum of progress met with resistance. After the Civil War, emancipation, and Reconstruction, Jim Crow laws imposed a new reign of terror on Black citizens. After the civil rights movement won basic freedoms, Nixon and Reagan gutted federal programs designed to legislate equality.

This book is dangerous. The work of antiracism is dangerous. And this conversation may be too. Why? Because some people are invested in the status quo—so invested that they see any discussion of the nature of that status quo, any questioning of its validity, as a threat to their status and their identity.

Discussing race at work is even more complicated, and uniquely threatening to one's identity. Like it or not, work is foundational to our lives, and not just because of the money. We identify ourselves through our occupations. Often the first thing we ask upon meeting someone is what they do for a living. It's a major determinant of our sense of self-worth. When you call attention to the fact that racism exists in the workplace, you complicate people's narratives about meritocracy, how they earned what they have, and their sense of themselves and their worth. You call into question one of the primary ways in which we define ourselves.

In response, some may choose to deny that their privilege really exists in the first place, or emphasize their own hardships in order to justify their actions. Research has shown that people from privileged groups feel better about themselves when asked to think about their own group's disadvantages.

Moreover, many White people aren't good at talking about race. They aren't because they don't have to be. Robin DiAngelo, author of *White Fragility*, frames this as a byproduct of insulation from race-based stress. White privilege insulates White people from race-based stress and encourages them to expect comfort in discussions about race. It also encourages them to think that just showing up to these conversations—doing the bare minimum—is enough to warrant praise. When that doesn't happen, discomfort triggers a range of defensive responses, from arguing and withdrawal to tears and retaliation.

Before going into the ways in which fragility manifests and how we can combat it, it's important to recognize that our racial identity can influence the type and severity of the resistance that we may receive. More often than not, because of competency bias (which favors other White people) and perceptions of identity threat (which disfavor non-Whites), White people respond differently to other White people when the topic of race comes up. Allies, the truth is this conversation is probably a lot less risky for you. This is where it becomes really important for you to use your privilege to protect others. POC, especially BIPOC, you may want to tread more carefully. Do whatever you can to make sure that you are not shouldering the risk of having this conversation alone.

COMMON MANIFESTATIONS OF DEFENSIVENESS

Your boss may display defensiveness and resistance in a variety of ways, both during the course of your conversation and after. It's important that you be aware of the risks and prepare yourself for potential backlash.

FRAGILITY

Popularized by Robin DiAngelo, the term "White fragility" refers to defensive reactions to the racial stress that's triggered when White people are asked to engage with racism. These defensive reactions may include emotional displays such as angry outbursts, tears, or argumentation.

Common examples of White fragility that I have encountered in my work include phrases like:

- "Not all White people..."
- "Why should I feel guilty for..."
- "What about reverse racism?"
- "Why do we have to be so divisive?"
- "We should leave politics outside of work."
- "I don't want to do this. This is stupid."

Fragility shows up in our work so often that we have to account for it in our process. Participants in my workshops have argued with the facilitator, accusing them of personal attacks. I often have to remind my team that while all feedback tells us something, not all of it is constructive. White fragility works to redirect the conversation, focusing it on White comfort in an effort to reassert White dominance and White control.

Critics of DiAngelo argue that her approach still centers Whiteness and spends too much time enjoining White readers to focus on self-reflection and improvement at the expense of more structural approaches. That said, as someone who has given many a diversity training and professionally engaged in more conversations about racism than I can count, the phenomenon that DiAngelo describes is very real and can be very disruptive.

While an emotional response to having difficult conversations is normal, you don't want this conversation about racism to turn into a conversation focused on comforting your boss. In professional environments, people of color are often pressured to close off their own emotions and take care of those who perpetuate or benefit from racism in order to avoid confrontation or conforming to stereotypes, like the "angry" Black woman or "fiery" Latina.

Tears and rage can be weaponized to derail important conversations about race. They turn attention away from racism and the needs of people of color and toward the White person expressing emotion, thereby reinforcing White dominance and White supremacy. And this kind of emotional outburst from your boss can have a detrimental long-term impact on your relationship. If you sense fragility coming your way, try the following.

Encourage self-affirmation. Defensiveness is a protective response to perceived threats to White identity. To counter it, some research suggests that self-affirmation can reduce defensiveness and even prejudice. What is self-affirmation? Anything that bolsters one's sense of self-worth. In the research context, self-affirmation took the form of soliciting a description of a personal success or ranking a list of positive personal values. When this affirmation exercise was done before participants received negative information about prejudiced actions performed by members of their group, like the mistreatment of Aboriginal children or the institution of discriminatory antiterrorism policies, they were less likely to defend the racist action and more likely to acknowledge culpability. You may be able to use a similar approach in your conversation with your boss. Leverage your relationship with your boss to encourage them to self-affirm prior to initiating the portion of your conversation about race. Getting people to

self-affirm about race, without getting into lawsuit terri-
tory, is advanced-level stuff that even I haven't quite mas-
tered. So, it's best just to keep it high-level. Before getting
down to the nitty-gritty, check in with the following questions.

- What did you accomplish this week?
- What are the things you value most as a leader?
- How do you see your values reflected in the work of our team?

Keep things in perspective. Without minimizing the
impact or the harm of racism, encourage your boss to
depersonalize the situation by considering the broader
context. In my conversations with people, I always remind them that in creating an antiracist workplace, we're
trying to do something that literally has never been done
before. Every organization that cares about combating
racism has struggled to get it right.

Take a learning position. Preempt perceptions of
threat and defensive responses by framing antiracist
action as an opportunity for learning and growth. Anti-

racism is a process, not a goal. There is no perfectly anti-racist organization. Acknowledging that fact and modeling humility in the conversation will go a long way toward disarming your boss's defensiveness.

Offer to take a break. If those approaches fail to prevent your boss from having a meltdown, offer to take a short break. Disrupt the dynamic, minimize distraction, and avoid the temptation of falling into a caretaker role. During this break, think carefully about whether you're prepared to keep going with this conversation. Your boss's emotional reaction may turn you into a target.

If you want to end the conversation, let your boss express the emotions they need to express, communicate that you have heard them, and move the conversation along. Try something like, "I hear you saying X. Maybe it makes sense for us to pause the conversation here and revisit it at another time."

DENIAL

Remember 2008, when America became postracial? Neither do I. Yet many, including White liberals with good intentions, insisted that the election of the country's first Black president meant that racism was no longer a serious problem deserving of the same level of consternation it had caused in the past. While many a White liberal "would vote for Obama for a third term if they could," this idea that the elevation of the country's first Black president also magically signaled the end of racism is perhaps one of the most high-profile recent examples of White denial. Black, White, or Brown, many Americans wanted to believe that Obama's election showed that we had turned a corner, despite evidence to the contrary. That starry-eyed optimism had consequences. The White denialism of the Obama era was particularly pernicious. In those eight years, the rollback of civil rights protections included state-level bans on affirmative action and the gutting of the Voting Rights Act of 1965.

Denial is a form of fragility that minimizes the severity and pervasiveness of racism, like downplaying the racist act you just experienced or socially pressuring people of color into minimizing their own experiences of racism to accommodate a "color-blind" worldview. In the workplace, denialism can manifest in a few ways:

- Denying the need to focus on race or framing conversations about race as an unnecessary distraction from real work.

- Placing the blame elsewhere. People love to blame the "talent pipeline" instead of acknowledging racist hiring practices or toxic working conditions that make it difficult to hire BIPOC talent and keep the employees that do make it through.

- Focusing on one relatively benign manifestation of racism while ignoring other, more pernicious kinds. The popularity of the unconscious bias framework is a great example. Rather than acknowledging overt interpersonal racism or institutional racism, many organizations have instead focused on unconscious bias as the primary driver of racial inequity, which has, as we discussed earlier, diverted attention from more impactful solutions.

- Rejecting that race or racism is the problem. Supposedly, race has nothing to do with it.

- Asserting color-blindness. Saying things like "I just don't see race."

As a Black person, I find denialism hard to swallow—harder than some of the other defensive responses we've discussed, because denialism, more so than any of the others, erases my identity and my pain in service of White comfort. And to me, being able to deny reality, simple *reality*, is the ultimate manifestation of privilege.

That said, though it's emotional, this defense mechanism is also probably one of the easiest to navigate in the workplace context, because many of the narratives rooted in denial can easily be disproven or dismissed. It's hard to blame the pipeline when most of your POC employees turn over in less than a year. Who cares if you're color-blind if your product's algorithmic bias harms Black customers? So lead with the objective facts: "Year over year, we've lost a higher percentage of POC employees than White ones; our racial diversity is far below the industry standard"; or "More POC customers have found the following issues with our product or platform." Build to the conclusion that you want your boss to come to.

Be warned, however, that you can have the most compelling facts in the world and still fail to convince your boss. Denial isn't rational. Denial, in fact, requires precisely that we ignore rationality or facts in order to treat others in a way that conforms to our worldview. Irrationality is rarely overcome through rational approaches. If your boss insists on keeping their head in the sand (or in a YouTube conspiracy hole), if they refuse to be convinced, you can't force them to see the light. It may be time to think about how to work around them or to find a new job. (More on that in chapter 9.)

DISTANCING

Not everyone reacts emotionally or irrationally to conversations about race. Some people just try to remove themselves from the conversation altogether. Distancing can look like shutting down emotionally during a conversation, tone policing, intellectualizing the issue, or shifting the focus of the conversation away from the person you are talking to toward others "who are really part of the problem."

I see this a lot in my work with polite White people who don't want to fully participate in conversations about race or interrogate their role in racist environments but also don't want to be seen as walking out of the conversation altogether. I also frequently encounter this response from folks who consider themselves allies or intellectuals but want to engage with racism on their own terms—for example, they want to address the issues of racism that they perceive but not the ones that POC tell them are the most urgent. Like denialism, distancing helps those with privilege maintain their worldview and reject information that may threaten their sense of identity. It can also function to absolve them of responsibility for solving the problem of racism. If they refuse to expose themselves to diversity or engage with challenging information about race, they don't have to do anything.

In addition to silence and disengagement, there are problematic narratives people tell themselves to distance themselves from conversations about race and racism. Some of the most common that I have encountered are:

"I'm not like those other White people. How do I help the White people who are the problem?" These are two sides of the same coin. The person acknowledges that racism is an issue. They might even engage in difficult conversations about race—but without examining their own privilege, complicity, or problematic behavior.

"Racism is a problem of the past, and it will die out along with older generations." The Proud Boys and the "very fine people" who marched in Charlottesville would beg to differ. Though racism has endured for generations

and generations, this kind of magical thinking frames it solely as a problem of the past that will just go away on its own. It ignores the research on racism in younger White people, which shows that while White children are less overtly racist White adults, they are more apathetic in the face of racism. It also ignores the durability of systemic racism. It's ageist, as there are plenty of older people who are antiracist and younger people who aren't. It justifies apathy: Why fight racism if it's just going to die out? And it absolves not just the individual in question but that individual's *entire generation* of any culpability or responsibility for solving the problem.

"Old White men are the problem." This is a sneaky one. I'm most likely to encounter it when I'm talking to White feminists. These women are all too happy to throw White men under the bus, but they never seem to get around to actually talking about their own relationship to White supremacy or racism in general. In fact, I most commonly hear this phrase in conversations where race isn't even on the table—like every panel on "women's issues" or "gender inclusion" prior to 2017. Then, I often heard how White men were a problem, but we never got around to talking about the role that racism or White

supremacy played in the marginalization of women, especially non-White women. This framing superficially acknowledges race in conversations about sexism (or homophobia or ableism) without actually addressing the ways racism and White supremacy function or the speaker's relationship to them. Naming a common enemy without delving into the intersectional nature of the problem establishes false solidarity.

So how do you get the person with whom you are talking to remain actively engaged and discourage them from blaming someone else for the racist issues you would like to address? Navigating distancing takes a little more finesse than confronting outright denialism. The key to overcoming it lies in engaging someone in a conversation that they really have no desire to be a part of, and that's not easy to do. However, there are a few conversational techniques which you may find helpful in this situation.

Contrasting. A technique described in *Crucial Conversations*, contrasting is a statement that reinforces psychological safety by addressing what the other person might worry that you're saying while clarifying your actual intent. For example, in a conversation with your boss you might say, "I don't for a second want you to come away with the impression that I think you personally are a racist, and I value your support as a manager. I've noticed that we haven't talked about the latest police shooting as a team, and I would like to discuss that with you."

Watch the other person and adjust your tone accordingly. You aren't going to railroad your boss into believing what you believe. Approaching this conversation from an overly forceful or argumentative place can alienate someone who you'd like to turn into an ally. You and I both know that racism is important and requires urgent action. Like me, you probably also hate the idea of coddling someone with privilege and refuse to have your tone policed by people who'd rather just shut down any conversation about racism. I get it. But you're also trying to persuade someone to adopt your point of view through discussion—which requires reading nonverbal cues and moderating your approach to encourage engagement.

Ask the right questions. Don't let this become a one-sided conversation by allowing the person whom you're talking to distance themselves. Demonstrate openness and encourage self-reflection by asking your boss questions that invite them to share their perspective. Make it clear that you are aware that their views may differ from yours but that you still want to hear them. Then allow them time to answer. Try asking, "How is this landing? How do you see this issue? How have you dealt with racism in the past?" Learn how to embrace, or at least endure, whatever awkward silence hovers there until your boss replies.

SEA LIONING

The term was coined to describe trolling on the internet, but it has gone mainstream. It's the bad-faith tactic of responding to an argument that one dislikes with persistent questions, requests for more data, or invitations to debate. Usually these are conveyed with politeness and faux sincerity, so that if the target of the questioning loses their temper, the questioner can act like the victim. Sea lioning is designed to exhaust the target's patience and energy while also portraying them as unreasonable. Over time it can erode trust, discouraging people from answering questions posed in good faith or engaging those with a genuine desire to learn.

I encounter sea lioning quite a bit in data-driven or

technical environments. People often ask me to make the business case for diversity, as though it hasn't been established for years, and press me for "proven solutions" that they can start implementing tomorrow. Every claim about discrimination must be supported by irrefutable data and every possible counter explanation for disparate outcomes must be explored and refuted before we assume that racial discrimination is the cause.

To be clear, I have no problem with educating or sharing knowledge with people. And I shouldn't; I built a business around it. But I also think it's important to be able to identify when you are engaging in conversation with someone who has no intention of learning. When you talk to your boss, it's important for you to be able to differentiate between well-intentioned questioning, or the reasonable expectation that you support your argument, and a bad-faith attempt to exhaust you with endless questions and requests for more research.

Signs that your boss might be sea lioning instead of generally engaging:

- They ask questions in rapid succession, without waiting for an answer.

- They miss the forest for the trees, focusing on details and small points of argumentation rather than the larger themes of the discussion.

- They ask questions whose answers are easily found.

- They keep moving the goalposts when you provide answers to their questions.

- They are quick to frame themselves as logical and rational, and you as irrational, emotional, unprepared, or unsophisticated.

Responding to sea lioning can be tricky because it's designed to gaslight you and goad you into exhaustion. However, there are a few things you can do to address it.

Come prepared. Remember all that work that we did in chapter 4? Use that. Have your argument polished and your sources ready. Be prepared to share them in the conversation with your boss and to follow up with further information or resources.

Focus on providing objective data. Use personal narrative and subjective interpretations sparingly. While those perspectives are valuable, they are relatively easy targets for someone who came looking to punch holes in your argument. That said, be honest with yourself about when the objective data isn't being heard. Sometimes repeated requests for data are more about exhausting you than engaging in a productive conversation. You don't have to fall down the rabbit hole.

Ask your boss clarifying questions. What kind of information would they find most useful? How do they see the issue? Where do they feel stuck? What do they think you might be missing?

RETALIATION

Sadly, there will always be those folks who are okay with the world as it is. There will always be people who believe that your activism poses a greater threat to your organization than its own racism. Trying to engage these people may do more harm than good and could make you a target.

Retaliation is conduct from your employer meant to punish you for bringing up issues of discrimination, and possibly also to deter you from doing it again. Retaliation can take the form of harassment, demotion, termination, or forcing you out by other means. It is illegal but quite common. In fact, the majority of workplace discrimination claims submitted to the Equal Employment Opportunity Commission (EEOC) were retaliation claims. One study found that more than 75 percent of people who spoke out against harassment experienced retaliation.

You should be aware that if you bring up the topic of race with your boss, they or your organization's human resources department may respond by trying to shut down the conversation, make an example of you, or get rid of you altogether.

So how do you protect yourself?

Document, document, document...and keep your documentation secure. We've mentioned this already, because it's so important. If you have observed racist behavior in the workplace, you should record details about the interactions you have seen, including who was involved, when the incident occurred, and its impact. Keep a record of the conversations that you have with your boss and always follow up by email to confirm what was discussed and the agreed-upon outcomes. Be careful about actually recording conversations without your boss's consent—in some states, that's a crime, and even if it isn't, it may be seen as a breach of workplace confidentiality. If your boss starts to treat you differently or evaluate your performance differently after your conversation, keep a record of that too. Remember that if your company owns your email, phone, or laptop, they can revoke access at any time. The more information you can (legally) store off of machines owned by your employer, the better.

File a complaint with the Equal Employment Opportunity Commission. The EEOC enforces federal laws that prohibit workplace discrimination and protect those who report discrimination from retaliation. At least, it is supposed to. The agency is woefully underfunded and overwhelmed. Since 1980, its budget has remained nearly flat, and the number of investigators on its payroll has declined, even as the number of workers and workforce complaints has increased. The agency faces a significant backlog, and the average time to resolve a private-sector complaint is nearly three hundred days. That said, the EEOC does investigate some cases and can help you get justice if you have been targeted. Some states also require that you file a complaint with the EEOC before obtaining the right to sue your employer.

Familiarize yourself with state labor laws and your

state workforce protection agency. The EEOC isn't the only agency tasked with protecting workers from discrimination; some state agencies offer protection for workers as well. Make sure you understand your state's labor protections. Depending on where you live, you might have better luck at the state level than the federal level.

Call on your allies. Work those relationships that we talked about creating in the previous chapters. If there is any way at all that you can get others to stand alongside you and voice similar concerns, you should. It's not a foolproof way to avoid being targeted—just ask the Google walkout organizers. But it can make it a lot harder for your company to single you out and can increase the scrutiny aimed at your colleagues' bad conduct.

Hire a lawyer. In my experience, a good lawyer is the best protection against gaslighting. If you have the means to do so, consult with an employment attorney as soon as you can. They can help you to understand whether the treatment you are experiencing fits the legal definition of retaliation and what your legal options are. They can also scare your employer into doing the right thing or agreeing to a settlement if you do separate. Please, please, please do not assume that hiring a lawyer is financially out of reach. Employers rely on employees being too intimidated by the legal system to defend their own rights. Many lawyers will offer you a free or low-cost consultation at the outset, and some will work with you to find a payment plan that aligns with your needs. I say this from experience: getting a lawyer to write a threatening letter for you can be a surprisingly cheap and effective way to get a bad-faith actor to back off.

File a complaint with HR (if they're not terrible). Full disclosure: This could actually make your problem worse (that's kind of why it's tacked on at the end here). Most HR departments are in the business of protecting the company's interests, not yours. Though you may luck out and find a department committed to creating an inclusive culture and protecting their employees, you're far more likely to have to deal with one that views vocal employees as troublemakers. Moreover, the folks in HR are just as likely to be biased as anyone else in your org. So, file a complaint. Create a paper trail. But be prepared for a complaint to escalate the situation.

Above all else, keep your head up. Resistance is a natural part of this work, one that many of us are woefully unprepared for.

We are taught to believe that the arc of history is linear and bends toward justice, that once society is shown the light it bravely marches toward it. That's a lie that keeps us comfortable. There has always been backlash to progress. Reactionary forces have always tried to undo the work of progressives. The more prepared we are to face these facts and the quicker we are to see backlash as part of a broader pattern, the more effective we can be as advocates.

7

FROM MODEL MINORITY TO AFFIRMATIVE ACTION TO PROBLEMATIC PIPELINES

UNDERSTANDING AND UNPACKING POPULAR MYTHS

f only we could fix the pipeline."

"Let's just start with women."

"We don't want to lower the bar."

When you work as a diversity advocate, one who actively acknowledges race, you get used to hearing these lines. They're often said to me with a bashful smile and a knowing glance, because I'm Black. They're then often followed by the reassurance that "diversity, including racial diversity, really matters," because the people spouting these trash takes can see the look on my face.

In the last chapter, we explored the ways in which people may push back against conversations about race and racism overtly and aggressively. But people can also push back against these subjects subtly by using common narratives as shields. These narratives are designed to undermine legitimate claims of racism and to excuse or reinforce White supremacy, while still allowing the person pushing them to maintain the appearance of giving a shit.

Narratives are important. When I give trainings on systemic racism, we spend quite a bit of time exploring the role of narratives in securing and spreading inequality. I first encountered this idea through Charles Tilly, in his book *Durable Inequality*. Tilly describes the mechanism of adaptation, a process by which people build practices, narratives, routines, and social relations around systemic inequality. People grow used to inequality and even acquire an interest in its maintenance. When it comes to inequality, Tilly argues, adaptation creates an additional cost—whether it's psychological or temporal or monetary—to change.

Racist narratives historically have been created to justify racist actions, suppress resistance, and cement hatred and bigotry. At work, we tell ourselves these stories to adapt to and justify the inequality that we see. Over time, and the more closely we identify with our jobs, our investment in these tales grows. They keep us from questioning too deeply and allow us to maintain the comfortable facade that exclusion is the natural outcome of a set of unchangeable conditions rather than an intentional, immoral choice.

In my line of work, I hear these stories all the time. Some of them used to trip me up. I believe that many of the people who spouted this problematic reasoning really believed what they were saying. I know that many of them considered themselves allies. But engaging with these ideas meant that I spent countless hours trying to navigate around paradigms designed to hold up racist institutions and practices. Which is why I'm writing this chapter—to save you some goddamned time.

Here are a few of the most common myths that I've

encountered so far in my career, and some helpful ways to combat them.

MYTH #1: "THIS IS A MERITOCRACY, AND WE DON'T WANT TO LOWER THE BAR"

The reasoning goes something like this:

At our particular company we don't try to actively exclude anyone. We're a meritocracy. We simply hire the best people. Yes, it's unfortunate that they all happen to be White bros named Chad, but we don't want to lower the bar. And though I am a White guy named Chad, I say this in the most unbiased way possible.

This, of course, is not true. Chad does not work in a meritocratic environment. He would like to believe he does, because this narrative justifies his presence. It buffers him from the threat to his identity that acknowledging his privilege would pose. But what working environment could be meritocratic when it is tied to biased systems (like our education system) and inhabited by biased individuals (which we all are)?

Chad's aspiration to meritocracy is founded upon a fairy tale—or, put more correctly, a dystopian satire about the future of Britain, where success is determined by an equation: merit = IQ + effort. The novel *The Rise of the Meritocracy* was written in 1958 by British sociologist and politician Michael Young. It was intended to highlight the dangers of classism and educational gatekeeping. Young coined the term "meritocracy" to describe a system in which the elite saw success as a just reward and pursued wealth accumulation without shame. Those left behind, they argued, were responsible for their own failures.

Today the idea of meritocracy has been stripped of all of its original satirical meaning. We now treat it as a desirable and achievable end. Toward the end of his life, Young lamented this development, stating:

> *The business meritocracy is in vogue. If meritocrats believe, as more and more of them are encouraged to, that their advancement comes from their own merits, they can feel they deserve whatever they can get.*
>
> *They can be insufferably smug, much more so than the people who knew they had achieved*

*advancement not on their own merit but be-
cause they were, as somebody's son or daughter,
the beneficiaries of nepotism. The newcomers
can actually believe they have morality on their
side.*

In reality, there are all sorts of biases that impact even
the most meritocratic workplace. As Young noted, education can stratify more than it equalizes. Racial segregation in US public schools continues to be a problem. Only
12 percent of White students attend schools that are
majority POC, while nearly 70 percent of Black students
do. Schools that are predominantly POC are also underfunded: 72 percent of all Black students attend a high-
poverty school, while only 31 percent of White students
do. Even where schools are integrated, Black and Brown
children face racism. Teachers' bias against Black students starts as early as preschool, where they are up to
four times as likely to be suspended and twice as likely
to be expelled. Access to higher education has also become increasingly restricted. The price of college has increased more than 25 percent in the last ten years, and
elite institutions like Yale, Brown, and Dartmouth take in

more students from the top 1 percent by income than the bottom 60 percent. Forty-three percent of the White students admitted to Harvard in 2019 were either athletes, legacies, or the children of donors or faculty. Bias can affect the quality of education you receive once you're in the door. Studies have shown that university faculty members are more likely to respond to emails from White male prospective grad students than any other demographic.

Our social networks, a form of alternative credentialing and the basis for preferential-referral hire schemes at many workplaces, are also biased. With little variance across geography, political affiliation, age, or gender, 75 percent of White Americans report that the only people with whom they discuss important matters are White.

And this is just the systemic stuff.

Individuals' biases that affect the workplace are harder to identify and control, but just as influential. Research has shown that workplaces that emphasize meritocracy actually have some of the most biased outcomes in hiring and performance evaluation. This phenomenon, discovered by researchers Dr. Emilio J. Castilla and Stephen Benard, is called the "paradox of meritocracy." Those who believe they are operating in an objective system are often the least likely to reflect on their behavior; the narrative of the meritocratic culture deludes people into thinking that they will behave fairly by default. The delusion of impartiality in the absence of active combat against bias in all its forms allows it to thrive.

But that's not the only reason Chad's assertion is horseshit. By equating diversity with "lowering the bar," Chad is implying that talent from other racial backgrounds is somehow "less than." He doesn't see antiracism or diversity as an improvement on the process, potentially increasing access to untapped talent; he sees it as a detriment. That's racist.

The indicators that we use to determine merit are often really flawed. Turns out interviews, schools attended, even past job experience can be really poor predictors of future performance. The foundations of most meritocratic workplaces are built on shaky ground indeed.

So how do you fight against this line of thinking?

- Reframe meritocracy as a shared goal rather than an outcome already achieved. One of my favorite lines is, "We all want meritocracy. But we're just not there yet. No organization is perfect, which

means there is plenty of opportunity for us to in-
novate to get there."

- Model humility to provoke humility. We're all on a
  learning journey.

- Advocate for achievable goals that still move the
  needle. Even if you don't have the power to do
  something dramatic, like overhauling your entire
  recruiting process; you can advocate for policies,
  processes, and programs that help level the playing field. Some examples: blind work sample tests,
  blind résumé screens, periodic third-party audits
  of your promotions and performance evaluation
  processes, sponsorship programming, and rewards
  for people who manage to achieve equitable outcomes on their teams.

MYTH #2: "RACIAL DIVERSITY IS IMPORTANT, BUT WE WANT TO AVOID AFFIRMATIVE ACTION, BECAUSE AFFIRMATIVE ACTION IS TERRIBLE"

I've been holding this one in for a while, and I know I'm about to piss a lot of people off. But I'm just going to say it: affirmative action isn't a bad thing.

Since I started my career in diversity and inclusion, there have been plenty of people who've said the opposite. "We want diversity," they say, "but how do we get it while avoiding affirmative action? No one wants affirmative action."

For years, I took that premise to be true. *No one wants affirmative action because it doesn't work and the harms it causes far outweigh the benefits.* Now, however, I think something closer to the opposite may be true: any approach to antiracism and increasing diversity within historically biased systems like the workplace *must* include elements of affirmative action. Affirmative action isn't perfect, but it's more effective than many other more popular approaches to increasing representation, like unconscious bias training or holding lots of events and panels to raise awareness.

First, let's talk about what affirmative action actually is. The term comes with quite a bit of baggage, so much so that many of those slamming affirmative action don't actually know what they are critiquing. The modern form of affirmative action was created by President John F. Kennedy's Executive Order 10925, establishing the Committee on Equal Employment Opportunity. According to the order, government contractors are required to

> take affirmative action to ensure that applicants are employed, and that employees are treated during employment, without regard to their race, creed, color, or national origin. Such action shall include, but not be limited to, the following: employment, upgrading, demotion or transfer; recruitment or recruitment advertising; layoff or termination; rates of pay or other forms of compensation; and selection for training, including apprenticeship.

Under his successor, President Johnson, federal contractors with fifty or more employees and federal contracts worth over $50,000 were also required to develop affirmative action plans.

That's it. Affirmative action isn't racial quotas; those are illegal. It's not hiring someone on the basis of their race or gender, which is also illegal. It's not giving special treatment to underrepresented folks. It's the requirement that federal contractors and agencies proactively ensure that workers not face discrimination.

And it works. Since it was enacted, affirmative action has increased representation for women and non-White workers, particularly African American and Native American workers. This increase in racial diversity persists even after firms stop contracting with the federal government and are no longer bound by affirmative action requirements. These improvements have taken place in both high-skilled and low-skilled occupations.

Many of the fears associated with affirmative action are ill founded.

Affirmative action doesn't lower the bar (again, such a racist premise). Research has shown that women and non-

White workers hired by organizations with affirmative action programs in place perform just as well on the job as their peers.

Affirmative action doesn't benefit some racial minority groups (like Black and Latino people) at the expense of others (like Asians). Though opponents of affirmative action frequently use the narrative that affirmative action negatively impacts Asian Americans, as a way to divide POC and pit groups against each other, affirmative action does not cap Asian representation. In fact, Asian representation in universities has increased since affirmative action was instituted. Today, nearly 70 percent of Asian Americans support affirmative action.

Affirmative action also isn't "reverse racism." White women also benefit from affirmative action. Some racial justice advocates insist that White women have actually been the primary beneficiaries of workplace affirmative action programs. White men haven't done so badly under affirmative action either. When it comes to college admissions, White men, who don't perform as well as their female counterparts in secondary education, benefit from affirmative action policies designed to maintain an equal gender ratio.

So why does affirmative action have such a bad reputation? A few reasons.

The first obviously has to do with racism. Some White people just don't like the idea of helping non-White people. This aversion has been reflected in the research, which has shown that White people's opinions are less favorable toward affirmative action when it is race-based or when it specifically benefits Black people.

The second, perhaps unsurprisingly, has to do with self-esteem. As we discussed in the previous chapter, acknowledging discrimination and privilege threatens the identities of those that benefit from them. Believing in a false idea of affirmative action, like racial quotas, makes some White people feel better about themselves. It reinforces the idea that they earned their position through merit (denying their racial privilege), while other groups didn't (creating the perception of racial privilege where it doesn't exist). Researchers found that this belief boosts White men's self-esteem by increasing their estimation of their own competence. The same has been shown for White women who don't think of themselves as beneficiaries of affirmative action. Believing in quotas makes them feel better about themselves.

I think it's important that we understand the nature of the affirmative action myth for two reasons: so that we can debunk it in the moment, and so that we gain a greater understanding of what actually works. Articulating goals about diversity, developing strategies to reach those goals, and being held accountable for the success or failure of the strategies are all elements of affirmative action programming that are associated with successful approaches to DEI overall. Beware of any pushback you get that tries to frame these approaches as something negative.

MYTH #3: "THIS IS A PIPELINE PROBLEM"

In 2015, I launched a newsletter that would change my life. It was called Hack the Network, and its premise was simple. I offered to advertise job openings at companies where my friends worked and had decision-making power to my diverse, "desirable" social network. I offered to pre-screen applicants for them, on the condition that once I introduced those applicants, they would be treated as internal referrals.

I mainly intended it as a favor to my friends. I invited folks to sign up to receive it with a Facebook post on my personal page and by posting to a few Meetup groups that I was a part of. I was woefully unprepared for the response. I heard from dozens of companies wanting to post their jobs and thousands of people looking to get on the distribution list.

In the email that I sent inviting folks to sign up, I accidentally left my phone number in the signature line. I started getting phone calls at all hours of the day from people desperate for jobs in tech. And they weren't who I thought of when I pictured the typical job seeker: Many had years of experience in tech roles. One had a PhD from Stanford. They came from all walks of life. The one thing they had in common, besides their desperation for work? They were all POC.

I started the newsletter because I sincerely believed in the pipeline myth. I thought the lack of racial diversity and racial equity in many companies, in the tech sector especially, was due to the limited number of qualified applicants for the roles advertised. I spent a lot of time and energy publishing that newsletter. It taught me a lot of valuable lessons, the most important of which was that the pipeline isn't the problem.

Yes, I will admit, in some fields, like technology, White and some Asian people are overrepresented relative to their share of college graduates. This overrepresentation can impact the pool of talent companies have to choose from in certain occupations. But those disparities don't explain the persistent lack of racial diversity in high-opportunity employment across most sectors in the job market, nor the stagnation or decline in representation in certain sectors. For example, take the legal field. The number of Black and Latino lawyers has remained virtually unchanged from 2010 to 2020 (at 5 percent and 4 percent, respectively), while the number of Native American lawyers has actually declined (from a measly 0.7 percent to 0.4 percent). Overall, African Americans and Latinos have seen extremely slow growth or declines in representation in professional and managerial roles.

Conversely, by many measures the pipeline has never been fuller. At all levels of higher education, the number of African American and Latino graduates has significantly and steadily increased. Over the past twenty-five years, the number of Black and Latino college graduates rose by 55 percent and 350 percent, respectively. Latinos make up around 17 percent of the working-age population, and African Americans make up around 13 percent. Relative to their percentage of the working-age population, African Americans and Latinos are actually overrepresented in the population of college graduates. The number of African Americans and Latinos receiving master's degrees has also risen significantly. The Latino share of master's degree graduates rose from 2 percent to 10 percent, and the share of African American graduates rose from 6 percent to 14 percent. Again, relative to their share of the working age population, they are overrepresented.

This educational attainment has not been reflected across professional spaces. Tech companies on average are around 3 percent Latino and 1 percent Black, even though 10 percent of computer science grads are Latino and 9 percent are Black. In law, we see the same trend. Despite record high employment in 2019, Black law students were hired into jobs requiring bar passage at a rate of 17 percent less than White law students. In general, Black and Latino college students get less for their degrees. On average, they earn less and are less likely than White and Asian graduates to be employed after graduation and to receive benefits at the jobs they do hold.

As we've discussed, the higher you get up the ladder, the more White it gets. Now, the pipeline apologists would have you believe that's just because there isn't enough diversity in the levels below. But again, the numbers tell a different story—a more racist story. The only group that has achieved or exceeded parity with their professional workforce at the executive level is White people. Every other group is drastically underrepresented. This is true even for non-White workers who are overrepresented in the professional workforce, like Asians, whose overrepresentation at the professional level isn't reflected at the executive level.

The pipeline story serves a very important purpose: it shifts the blame for the lack of diversity and representation away from the company to society at large. This makes it harder not just to hold the company accountable but to hold *anyone* accountable for a particular organization's low levels of representation. It also makes the people who work there feel better about their employer. It's a lot easier for a person to condemn society at large than to wrestle with working for a racist employer. Finally, it feeds into the reasoning that groups that are discriminated against are in some way more responsible for combatting discrimination than the people who do the discriminating. Taken to its logical conclusion, if the problem is the pipeline and not the organization, people of color just have to persevere and excel enough, pull on those bootstraps hard enough, and they'll make it in and thrive. When that doesn't happen, there is no reason for the organization to look inward.

People often focus on hiring in discussions about racial diversity and equity. They see representational diversity in the pipeline as the solution to racism and racial disparities. Representation can be helpful, but it's not a panacea. Without deeper reform and introspection, people from underrepresented backgrounds get worn down by racist behaviors, processes, and outcomes, and they leave. Representation does not equal access. Representation does not equal power. Building an antiracist organization requires that you do more than hire people. Very diverse organizations can still be racist ones.

I would even go so far as to say the concept of a pipeline itself is somewhat flawed. If an Ivy League education and specific, relevant job experience don't predict success on the job, why rely on those channels for recruiting or as indicators of competency?

Like the other myths, you can fight the pipeline myth with data (and I just gave you some). But I would caution against engaging with it on its own terms. The pipeline discussion keeps us stuck in the paradigm of representation as equity. The best way to combat the pipeline narrative is to move beyond conversations about simply hiring more people toward topics like retention and advancement, where failure cannot simply be explained away by the pipeline.

MYTH #4: "TO BE SUCCESSFUL, WE SHOULD START WITH WOMEN"

Let me just say that it's not a contest. (If it is, I would like to lose this contest, please.) Sexism sucks. Racism sucks. As someone who has to deal with both, and often at the same time, I can say that both are uniquely terrible. That said, every time a company comes to me and says, "We really care about diversity, but we just want to start with women," I bristle. Because I know what they're really saying. *Racism is too hard (or controversial, or deeply entrenched, or uncomfortable), so we're just going to focus on White women.*

Those who pose this argument in good faith sincerely believe that it's best to try to get diversity right with an "easier" group before moving onto groups that experience more "difficult" forms of marginalization. They believe an "easy win" will enable them to establish a successful track record and get greater buy-in for future attempts to level the playing field within their organization. Others see their daughters and wives in the struggle for gender equality and can't help but be driven to move the needle for them. Their ability to identify with certain women and their compassion for them keep them motivated to fight for equality even in the face of resistance.

Because a women-only approach is explicitly devoid by design of race or other complicating factors, it's most effective for a very small subset of women—those who align most closely with the default, who tend to have the most privilege: White women.

The "women first" argument is the trickle-down theory of diversity and inclusion. It's predicated on self-serving beliefs about benevolence and altruism, assuming that improving working conditions for one group will naturally improve them for everyone regardless of that group's complicity in White supremacy or racial privilege. It usually deepens privilege for one group with the expectation that this expansion of privilege will translate into a universal benefit. It never does. It fails to take into account that White women benefit from White supremacy and from aligning themselves with White men in power. For these reasons, it's not uncommon for organizations that employ a "women first" mindset to actually see worse outcomes for their Black and Brown employees.

Prior to 2020, when the global pandemic forced many women to downshift their careers or exit the workforce completely, women had made significant gains in the workforce. They were the majority of college graduates and had increased their representation in prestigious spaces like technology, law, medicine, and finance. Though it's not at parity, female representation has also increased in leadership roles.

These gains, while encouraging, primarily benefited White women. In tech, since 2014, companies like Facebook have increased representation of women in technical roles to 23 percent, up from 15 percent, as the number of Black employees has hovered steadily at less than 2 percent. In corporate America overall, one in five C-suite leaders were women, while only one in twenty-five were women of color. In some sectors, like technology, the share of women in leadership and management roles increased while representation for people of color at those levels declined.

Today, the picture is a little bit different. The global coronavirus pandemic has hit women from all backgrounds particularly hard. Women were more likely to be laid off or furloughed during the crisis. Of those still employed, more than a quarter have considered downshifting their careers or leaving the workforce altogether. But women of color felt these challenges more acutely. Black women in particular were more likely to be negatively impacted by the epidemic and less likely to receive support from their managers and colleagues.

It will take some time for women to recover from the losses they've incurred. As organizations begin to address these losses, I expect that we may see a resurgence of this "women first" narrative. Yes, we need to acknowledge the unique challenges faced by women in the workforce. But we need to balance it with support for other, less visible groups who deal with similar challenges exacerbated by historical inequity.

Instead of focusing on the least impacted groups because their challenges may be easier to solve, let's identify the needs of the most impacted groups, whose issues are more likely to reflect deeper structural problems and who may feel organizational pain points earlier that eventually affect everyone.

Ultimately, however, I never suggest that diversity efforts "start" with any group. Nor should they be segmented by group at all. It's almost impossible to change an organizational culture for one group at a time or to develop a cohesive strategy for one group. When organizations try to do this, they tend to embed practices that ignore intersectionality and leave large parts of their employee population behind. Eventually, many organizations that employ the "one group first" or the "one group at a time" approach just keep undoing work and reinventing the wheel until they exhaust themselves out of doing anything at all.

A helpful way to counter the "let's start with women"

narrative is by reminding others that it just creates more work in the long run. By tackling bias holistically, with an understanding of sexism, racism, anti-gay and anti-trans bias, ageism, ableism, and other forms of discrimination, we're more likely to create solutions that work better for those with intersectional marginalization and improve the culture as a whole. This holds true for racism too. Black and Brown people are not a monolith. Women of color, trans and nonbinary people of color, queer people of color, and people of color with disabilities all fare particularly badly in many organizations. To ensure that we support all people of color, we must holistically acknowledge their identities and these other marginalizations as well.

MYTH #5: "THIS IS AN AMERICAN PROBLEM. ANTIRACISM DOESN'T APPLY IN THE GLOBAL CONTEXT"

When I worked in Brussels, I used to walk by a statue of King Leopold every day on the way to work. He's responsible for the deaths of as many as ten million Congolese men, women, and children. He was a man so racist and evil, his reign inspired the phrase "crimes against humanity." He's memorialized all over the city in bronze.

The last time I was called the n-word was while walking back to my hotel after dinner in Amsterdam. Several years later, in that same city, I talked to a young Black lawyer from Curaçao, who confided in me about the racism and denialism he faced at work every day.

In Panama, I was searched by police dogs everywhere, wherever they happened to be. Just me.

Remember that consulting firm I told you about in chapter 5? That was a French consulting firm operating in Afghanistan. In the conversation where I confronted them about their racism, one of the partners said (and I shit you not): "Y-Vonne, maybe it's your American perspective. We just don't have racism in France like you do there. Like, sometimes we call Black football players monkeys and throw bananas at them. But for us, that's not racist."

(Dear reader, it is. In fact, it is EXTREMELY racist to throw bananas at Black people and call them monkeys.)

In my life and in my work, I have been told a multitude of times by White people around the world that racism, particularly anti-Black racism, is a uniquely American problem. Sometimes this happens with companies with an international presence. Other times, it's used as justification by companies based abroad who want to work with us, but only if we look at inclusion only for specific groups (usually women). My lived experience and the experiences of others from ethnic minorities that I have encountered around the world indicates there's nothing special about America. Just as colonialism was global, so too is its cousin, racism.

These observations are backed by research. In France, job applicants with Arab-sounding last names receive 25 percent fewer responses than those with French-sounding last names. In Brazil, the average income for White workers is 74 percent higher than that for Black and Brown workers. In Japan, 38 percent of foreign workers report discrimination in the workplace.

Globally, the economic costs of racism are significant. Though numbers at a regional and international level are hard to come by, country-level data gives us some indication of the magnitude. As I've already mentioned, racism has cost the United States $16 trillion. France could boost its economy by $3.6 billion over the next twenty years if it eliminated racial disparity in employment and education. It is believed that racism cost the Australian economy 44.9 billion Australian dollars between 2001 and 2011.

Unfortunately, in many of these countries, racial denial plays a powerful role in discouraging conversations about racism. In France, the national mythology of "liberty, equality, fraternity" leads many to argue that their society is color-blind. The country's legal prohibition against collecting data based on race reinforces this delusion. In Japan, claims of racial naivete and inexperience with societal diversity undermine the conversation. In Brazil, the myth of peaceful multiracial democracy masks systemic racial inequality and impedes movements for racial justice.

Globally, racial denialism functions the same way as it does in the United States: It gaslights the victims into believing their marginalization isn't real. It also protects the majority group's sense of identity. Similarly, it should also be combated with data and arguments that emphasize the immediate benefits of fighting racism, like avoiding scandal or increased competitiveness in a tight labor market.

In the international context, it helps to acknowledge

that the historical drivers and targets of racism may differ from country to country. For this reason, a focus on impact can also be helpful. Racism in Singapore isn't the same as racism in Brazil or France, but the effect on racially marginalized groups is remarkably similar—limited opportunity, labor-market segregation, and unfair treatment at work.

In all likelihood, you may encounter at least one of these myths in your conversation with your boss. Sadly, even people you consider allies might believe one of these myths. Though diversity work is not new, misconceptions about it have been allowed to persist because corporate approaches to diversity have traditionally been neither rigorously empirical or interested in challenging the status quo.

This is, of course, where you come in.

8

WALK THE WALK

MOVING FROM
CONVERSATION TO ACTION

I n advocacy work, there is a school of thought, predicated on a very optimistic view of the human race, that once you have the tough conversation and do the hard work of educating those who need to be educated, change will follow.

This is called "raising awareness."

Nowadays, people love raising awareness. They do it with hashtags on Twitter, infographics on Instagram, panels at conferences, and difficult conversations at work. Sadly, the activism ends there for many. So does the progress.

Raising awareness as a behavioral change strategy has limited effectiveness. From healthcare to crime prevention to environmental protection, research has shown that providing information alone is not enough. When done poorly, it can actually increase the likelihood that someone will engage in the very activities you wish to prevent. Take a study focused on theft deterrence at Arizona Petrified National Forest National Park. Researchers found that visitors who were presented with information about the high levels of theft from the park were actually more likely to steal wood than those who weren't, because the awareness of bad behavior normalized it.

It turns out people make decisions for all kinds of reasons, including but by no means limited to a lack of awareness about the impact of those decisions. Pursuit of power, self-validation, social acceptance, short-term pleasure: all of these can influence the choices we make about how we treat others and the behaviors we accept, perhaps far more than our awareness about our impact.

Beyond the traps of raising awareness, organizations are vulnerable to what some call the "knowing-doing gap." Identified by Jeffrey Pfeffer and Robert Sutton, this is the phenomenon of employees knowing too much and doing too little, while substituting discussion and knowledge acquisition for action. The knowing-doing gap is particularly pernicious in workplaces because it's often tempting to measure impact in the short term. It's much easier and faster to measure the quantity and quality of talk than the quality of behavioral solutions and organizational reform, as Pfeffer and Sutton point out.

Sustainable cultural and behavioral change can take months, if not years, to materialize. That time scale doesn't work for many organizations that are looking to demonstrate success immediately. So they overemphasize conversation as a way to demonstrate impact.

I see the limits of conversation quite a bit in my work. People will reach out to hire us and say, "We've had the roundtable. We've had the training. We've had the difficult conversations. Now what?"

Providing information alone isn't enough. Conversation itself rarely solves the problem. In work, as in life, actions speak louder than words.

As we have crucial conversations about race at work, it's important that we consider how they can be reinforced with action. It can be difficult to figure out how to take action within a powerful system as an individual. At ReadySet, we talk about moving from allyship as an identity to an active practice. The following are actions that you can take at an interpersonal or systemic level to start the practice of addressing racism in your workplace.

Some of these suggestions will require the support of your manager, but many won't. Many you could start doing tomorrow. Yes, conversation is important. But you don't have to wait for it to make a difference.

INTERPERSONAL ACTIONS

At this point in the book (and after a not insignificant amount of profanity), it may surprise you to learn that I am an optimist. I do this work because I believe the possibility of change and I believe in the powers of individuals to make that change. That change starts with the actions we chose to take. I tell my team and my clients (and often myself) that every day offers us a chance to do something different, to take one little step that may make someone's day or change their lives.

If you find yourself asking the question "What can I

do?" the answer is often "Start small." Start with what's in your control. Build up those muscles. Train for the battle with Goliath. Make sure that you are walking your talk. Here are a few ways to do that.

CONTINUE TO EDUCATE YOURSELF

I know we've said it quite a bit in this book, but self-work and self-education are a huge part of doing antiracism work. It's the only way to make sure that you aren't part of the problem that you seek to resolve. Always remember that antiracism is a practice, a journey. If there is a destination, we haven't reached it yet. Stay engaged. Invest in yourself. Never stop learning.

Don't ask people to answer questions that you easily can Google. Pay attention to emergent issues that may be traumatic or emotionally fraught for your colleagues. Expose yourself. Diversify your social network and treat the people in it with respect. When they offer their perspectives, listen, but don't tokenize them or ask them for free emotional labor. As you continue your learning journey, pay special attention to the things that make you uncomfortable. That discomfort may shed light on areas that you need to work on. This is true for my fellow POC out there too. We aren't exempt from racism. Learn about and unpack the racism that exists in your community.

ADDRESS RACISM WHEN YOU SEE IT

Bystanders have a lot of power. Our workplace cultures and standards of behavior are created not on paper but by the everyday actions we use to build relationships, set boundaries, and get our jobs done. When we let acts of racism slide, large or small, we say this behavior is acceptable. We say that the impact that racist behavior has on our coworkers is acceptable too. Over time, these practices and ways of communicating harden into norms that become harder to uproot.

Culture aside, there is also a personal cost. Take it from me: experiencing harassment or microaggressions while colleagues you know, trust, and even consider to be your friends do nothing is a special kind of torture. When I think of the racism that I have experienced throughout my career, the instances where people watched it happen—

where they watched me get berated or ignored, made fun of or passed over—and failed to act are the ones that stick with me. Quite often they were also the tipping points, the pivotal moments where I said, "Fuck this job. Fuck these people," and I fully detached. Sure, I'd do my job. But I wasn't going to go the extra mile for those people and I certainly wasn't going to let them in.

It was in those moments that I saw that people were okay with my pain. Those moments confirmed my deepest fear—that I was on my own. The same woman who thanked me for speaking up for her in a meeting would never return the favor. The folks who relied on me for emotional support couldn't be depended upon to return it. No matter how good I was at my job, I would still, on some level, be expendable.

If you ever hope to contribute to building an equitable workplace as an ally, you will eventually have to confront and disrupt racist behavior. The more power your social identity carries, the better placed you are to intervene and the more responsibility you have to do so. Remember, racist behavior isn't always obvious or overt. Not every racist colleague is going to make a terrible joke or write a manifesto about how White people are naturally inclined to make more money.

Racism at work is more likely to manifest through a pattern of microaggressions and subtle behaviors like talking over someone, ignoring their contributions, giving them unfavorable reviews, excluding them from plum assignments or social activities, and gaslighting them when they do speak up for themselves.

Overt or covert, it comes to interrupting racism, you have to think strategically. Keep the following in mind:

Call it out in the moment. When you are dealing with colleagues who possess similar power as you within the organization, and where it seems productive, you can interrupt problematic behavior in the moment. You can do this directly or indirectly. One of my favorite indirect tactics is just to ask the person who says something foul to repeat themselves. Ironically, that can shut someone up really quickly. When it comes to direct engagement, I recommend focusing on the content of the message and why it was harmful rather than the person's character. Keep it short and concise and focus on values. An easy phrase to remember that embodies this approach: "We don't do that here."

Keep in mind that with this technique, as with most things, context matters. Your position in an organizational hierarchy, your relationships, the people around you, and the types of social power you hold will affect your ability to speak up without getting fired. Calling out behavior is easier and more effective with your peers and those who report to you. It's probably not a good idea to tell your boss, "We don't do that here" in the middle of a meeting with all of their direct reports. When you need to address the behavior of your boss or someone with more power than you, other techniques might be more effective.

Take the person aside. When there's more of a power differential or you feel like calling the person in would make a real difference in their behavior, pull them aside to discuss their actions. Here, as with direct intervention, the same recommendations apply. You can also lean into education, sharing a bit about your own journey and guiding the person toward resources.

Get consent before escalating. Keep in mind that your intervention could result in greater harm for the target of racism (if it's not you), particularly if intervening escalates the situation. In situations where this seems likely, be sure to get the consent of the person being targeted before you jump in to intervene.

Don't ask the target to do emotional labor for you. Chances are the person who is experiencing racism knows it's fucked up. You don't have to reach out to them to tell them that. You also don't want to get into a situation where the person suffering harm has to emotionally support you, the person who witnessed it. By all means, reach out to your coworkers who have experienced racism and offer your support. Ask them what they need. Offer options. Then be ready to do the heavy lifting.

Avoid humor. You've probably noticed that I joke around quite a bit in this book. I can do that because I'm funny and I'm Black. Humor is how I cope with *my* oppression. If you are not a member of the group being targeted at that moment, I do not recommend trying to de-escalate a situation by cracking a joke. It may seem like you are ratcheting down the intensity of a particular interaction, but you also risk making light of someone's very real oppression. You also risk communicating that a situation that is very serious, isn't. It's not worth it.

Engage in sponsorship. Notice I didn't say "mentorship." Mentorship is important. But many POC have mentors up the wazoo, and not all of them are helpful. Mentors are meant to teach and advise, often by sharing from their own experiences. That can be nice, but you can't mentor someone out of their own oppression.

Instead, or in conjunction, consider engaging with potential mentees as a sponsor. Research shows that working Americans who have a sponsor at work are paid on average 11.6 percent more than those who don't. They are also more likely to advance more quickly in their careers. Sponsors actively promote the work of the people they support and create opportunities for them to succeed and be recognized for their effort. Like mentors, sponsors offer feedback and advice. But they also leverage their privilege to advocate for and position those they sponsor.

Some organizations have formal sponsorship programs. But even if yours doesn't, you can informally develop a sponsorship relationship with a less senior colleague.

Think about the power you hold. Who do you have access to? What rooms do you find yourself in? Where are you considered an insider? Now think about those who are less senior than you. Who could benefit from that access?

Do avoid falling into the trap of "like me" bias. While you want to sponsor someone who can benefit from your unique experience and who is facing some of the same challenges you have, sponsorship across differences can be valuable too. For example, research shows that women who are sponsored by men earn higher salaries than those who aren't, because men have more power within organizations. Similarly, Black and Latina women who have sponsors of the same race make less than those with White ones. As you craft these relationships, keep in mind the unique challenges that your sponsees may face as a result of the identities that they hold.

Amplify the voices of marginalized people. You don't have to be a sponsor to ensure that your marginalized colleagues are equally given visibility and recognition. You can amplify the voices of your colleagues in everyday interactions. Make sure they are in the room. Encourage them to participate in discussions, and reorient the conversation toward them when they get talked over. Make sure that they aren't disproportionately tapped to take on duties that would inhibit their participation, like note taking, especially if those duties aren't in their job description. Make certain they receive credit for their ideas. Publicly celebrate them when they do good work. When advocating for inclusion, avoid speaking on behalf of people whose identities you do not share, and be mindful of when you may be centered at their expense.

HOW TO CHANGE THE SYSTEM

While it's a good start, working on an interpersonal level alone isn't enough to disrupt racism in any particular professional environment. As you know by now, racism and racist outcomes become embedded within organizations at the systemic level. Because of the way we value work in this country and the factors that influence access to high-opportunity employment, every workplace is in some ways influenced by systemic bias.

To combat this influence, it's important that we advocate at the systemic level within our places of work, but also that we leverage the power we have to change the inequitable systems that create biased and racist outcomes in the workplace.

Seem like a big job? Well, it is. But there are a few

places where you can start. As my mom likes to say, "How do you eat an elephant? One bite at a time." While I hesitate to compare undoing centuries of racism and White supremacy to eating an endangered pachyderm, I do think that reminding ourselves that this is a deliberate, step-by-step process can keep us from getting overwhelmed.

IMPROVE ACCESS TO INFORMATION

I always say that bias thrives in ambiguity. Bias flourishes where there can be plausible deniability, where only the insiders know, where there can be an alternative explanation, where victims can be gaslit into believing otherwise. One of the best ways to create ambiguous environments is by withholding information.

When exacerbated by bias, information asymmetry can create all sorts of disparate outcomes, from lower hiring rates (for those who may not know how to signal culture fit) to lower pay (for those who lack the data to effectively negotiate) to slower advancement (for those who may not have insider access or know how to navigate office politics). Access to information can decrease these gaps.

So give away all of the inside knowledge you can. Make things as transparent as possible for your colleagues of color and people of color whom your company may hire. Talk about the unwritten rules. Share your salary and negotiation tips. Share advancement opportunities. Help people find the resources they need to do their jobs better. Share your techniques for being seen and getting access (understanding that if you are White, the same approaches might not work as well for your POC colleagues).

FORM OR SUPPORT THE FORMATION OF AN EMPLOYEE RESOURCE GROUP

Employee resource groups (ERGs) are voluntary groups inside of a company formulated to support those who are members of a particular identity group. The first corporate ERG was launched at Xerox in 1970 to support the organization's Black employees after the social unrest of the 1960s. Now more than 90 percent of Fortune 500 companies have them. ERGs have historically served an important purpose in corporate organizations. They increase recruiting resources, improve retention, offer employee education opportunities, develop leaders, and create a sense of belonging for employees from under-represented and marginalized groups. All of these up-sides translate into quantifiable financial benefits.

Keeping this in mind, my recommendation to form or support an ERG is a tricky one that requires a few cave-ats. That's because while ERGs serve a noble purpose, in practice they also come with drawbacks. The first and most significant is the fact that with few exceptions, ERGs run on free labor. Employees from marginalized groups, who are often already under more scrutiny, are expected to do more work without additional compensation. And this extra work rarely translates into upward mobility. In fact, it may even damage career growth, since many organizations also fail to formally recognize ERG work as a contribution with quantifiable impact. Also, organi-zations can become overly reliant on ERGs to create an inclusive culture and delay allocating resources, hiring personnel with expertise, or establishing accountability for culture work.

So, by all means, push for and support employee resource groups, but do so mindfully. If you want to support ERGs as someone outside of their target group, I would absolutely encourage you to leverage some of your privilege on their behalf and advocate for and support them in a way that centers their work. So, whether you are a White ally or a person of color, how do you support equitable ERGs?

Help secure an executive sponsor. Use your connections or influence to identify and connect an executive sponsor, with substantial institutional power, to groups that may benefit from their support. Keep in mind that executive sponsors don't necessarily have to share the identity of the ERG that they are championing. It's more important that this person serve as a strong advocate that helps increase visibility and attract resources to the group.

Advocate for compensation. ERG work is real work. It should be valued as such. Resist those who expect you or your colleagues of color to work for free. In addition to compensation, push for a budget for the group itself. Otherwise, it's almost certain that the group members (who, thanks to pay inequity, almost certainly make less) will have to pay out of pocket or beg for resources to support their work. All of that impact doesn't come cheap.

Amplify the contributions of your ERG-running colleagues. Just as you would amplify the wins of your colleagues elsewhere, do so here. Make sure that your colleagues are publicly recognized for the very real positive impact that they are having on your culture. Push back when this work is framed as extracurricular or not core to the business. When you can, make sure recognition for it is included in your peer reviews.

ADVOCATE TO BRING IN THE EXPERTS

I can't tell you how many companies come to ReadySet because their employees pushed hard at a grassroots level for them to bring in the experts. We, in turn, advise nearly all of them to bring on expertise in-house. So many people want to believe that diversity, equity, inclusion, and antiracism work is intuitive, that anyone with enough passion can do it. But I assure you that it isn't and not everyone can. If anything, it's the opposite.

Doing this work effectively requires that we unlearn and fight against everything that our society sets as a default, because our default is racism. Moreover, understanding how these dynamics play out in organizations, what strategies are most effective to combat them, and why certain approaches won't work takes dedicated study. Knowing how to navigate all of those organizational dynamics takes experience. Dealing with *all the feels* takes skill. Hence, experts.

CONSIDER COMMUNITY IMPACT, NOT JUST COMMUNITY ENGAGEMENT

When many organizations think about corporate social responsibility at the community level, they frame their work as community engagement and relationship building. But rarely does this engagement look like truly participatory decision making. Instead, it usually consists of donations and one-off volunteer opportunities. Often it looks more like charity than the development of an equitable relationship.

The reality is that the products and services our

employers offer aren't neutral. Sometimes they can hurt people. The harm can be direct or even the result of flagrant negligence, like how social media companies ignored the problem of online harassment, which disproportionately harms users of color, or how the manufacturing industry largely ignored the issue of environmental pollution, which disproportionately harms Black and Brown communities. Harm can also be indirect, as through economic displacement driven by gentrification. The bottom line is that businesses can exacerbate systemic racism in the vulnerable communities that they touch.

Consider rideshare companies like Lyft, which are made up of mainly White and Asian corporate workers and a pool of more vulnerable drivers who are predominantly Black and Brown. Rideshare companies fought for these drivers to be classified as essential workers during the pandemic, so that they would be prioritized for vaccine access (which itself isn't bad), while also shelling out over $200 million to fight against legislation that would have reclassified them as employees and provided them better access to benefits like healthcare in states like California. To put it another way, rideshare companies were pushing to have drivers viewed as essential employees, while also effectively fighting to restrict their access to benefits, like healthcare in a global pandemic—a stance that was hypocritical at best and cynically exploitative at worst. When it looked like workers would be classified as employees, the rideshare companies threatened to cut their services during the pandemic. At the same time, Lyft and Uber advertised programs for the benefit of the community, like donations to charity and free rides.

One way to avoid creating harm is by listening to the communities impacted by organizations and incorporating them into certain decision-making processes. While you may not have the power to form a corporate-community board, you can deepen your personal relationship and engagement with communities impacted by your work. You can also bring community perspectives into the work that you do and help others recognize their impact. Bring in members from impacted communities to speak to your team, or better yet, hire them. At ReadySet, we've developed assessment tools for our clients to measure community harm. You can do something similar.

UNIONIZE

As we discussed in chapter 3, the best way to combat expansive corporate power is through collective action. While their record is mixed, unions historically have been used to combat workplace discrimination. Today, we're seeing a resurgence in unionization as a tool to protect workers who hold marginalized identities.

The Alphabet Workers Union, made up of Google employees and contractors and formed in response to repeated instances of retaliation and discriminatory action at the tech giant, is one example. Advocating for inclusion, fighting discrimination, and combating systems of oppression is baked into their mission statement, which proclaims,

> *We will use our reclaimed power to control what we work on and how it is used. We will ensure our working conditions are inclusive and fair. There is no place for harassment, bigotry, discrimination, or retaliation. We prioritize the needs and concerns of the marginalized and vulnerable. Workers are essential to the busi-*

ness. The diversity of our voices makes us stronger.

You, too, can form a union.

First and most importantly, you'll need to be sneaky. Typically, managers don't like unions. And while it's illegal to retaliate against unions, your employer can find all sorts of ways to get around (or just flagrantly ignore) that legal prohibition.

Next, talk to your colleagues. See if they share your concerns. Identify your most pressing issues. Gauge whether they're fired up enough to do something about it. Do not have these conversations on company time, using company devices, or within view of management. You don't want to tip them off this early in the game.

Then, contact a union organizer. You want to do this early, to create an extensive paper trail and have an advocate who knows the ins and outs as soon as possible.

Figure out which union is right for your organization. If you work in tech or media, it could be the Communications Workers of America. If you're an office worker, it could be the Office and Professional Employees International Union. Check the list of affiliated unions maintained by the AFL-CIO to find the union that might be the right fit.

Some organizers suggest that you also appoint a representative organizing committee to help you reach your coworkers and build support. Either way, you'll work with an organizer to send in National Labor Relations Board (NLRB) cards or a petition demonstrating the support of 30 percent of an organization. Once you've done that, with help from the NLRB, you'll hold an election in which hopefully more than 50 percent of your organization votes to support a union. Finally, you'll sign a contract.

Along the way, once management learns what's going on (likely when you start to reach out to the broader employee base), you can anticipate significant pushback: anti-union sessions, employee surveillance, lawyers, layoffs, and corporate restructuring. Fun times.

The path to unionizing isn't easy for a reason. Companies are scared of unions because they have the potential to disrupt control and shift the balance of power. Many of us, for whatever reason, think of unions as dying artifacts or a system exclusively for tradesmen. That doesn't have to be the case. Your rights as a worker include working in a place free of discrimination. Where companies fail to respect that right, and government enforcement of antidiscrimination law is weak, unions can be a powerful resource.

COMMON MISTAKES

I have yet to meet the perfect antiracist. We're all born into a racist society and indoctrinated into racist ideas. Undoing those influences can take a lifetime. That's why it's important to see this work as the journey that it is and to accept that we all make mistakes. That said, some mistakes are more avoidable than others. I, your handy dandy author, am here to help keep you from making them. Below are some common pitfalls to avoid.

FEEL-GOOD APPROACHES TO ANTIRACISM

As we've discussed, the first thing everyone wants to talk about when you bring up racism is unconscious bias. People love that conversation because it's an easy one to have. Unconscious bias lets you have racism without racists. The only problem: efforts focused on unconscious bias, like training, don't really work. The same can be said for efforts that overindex on White guilt, like the privilege walk, an exercise that helps White people understand their privilege by creating literal distance between them and less privileged people in the room. Folks with privilege tend to love a privilege walk, because it "opens their eyes." But this eye-opening moment often comes at the expense of those with marginalized identities; the exercise typically requires them to share their pain and sit with the lack of privilege they have so others can learn. Confronting racism will be uncomfortable for those with racial privilege. Instead of centering them and their discomfort, focus on the needs of those who are marginalized. Prioritize interventions that actually work, including ones we've discussed—creating strategies to tackle systemic outcomes, disrupting racist behavior, creating accountability, and sponsorship.

AD HOC APPROACHES WITHOUT STRATEGY

When you are working without institutional support, it can be tempting to do what you can to promote racial inclusion at work—an African American History Month panel here, a brown-bag session about more inclusive hiring there, and maybe a book club for good measure. While all of this programming may help you feel like you are being productive, it could be damaging. If you're not addressing the underlying causes of racism at work, it could feel performative to those affected. If your approach lacks direction or isn't driven by quantifiable impact, these efforts may burn people out, as they put in the effort without seeing results. Even at the grassroots level, it's important to have some kind of strategy associated with the antiracist work that you are doing. Work with ERGs or your diversity committee to gain a greater understanding of employee needs, then do what you can to address those, understanding there will only be so much you can do without resources and leadership buy-in.

OVERRELIANCE ON YOUR COLLEAGUES OF COLOR

I've said this already, but I think it's worth a reminder: Be aware of how much you are asking your colleagues of color to do. Yes, you want to center their perspectives and address their needs. But you shouldn't expect them to want to lead this work or to have time to educate you. You should also remember that quite often, the POC workers in your organization are under more scrutiny than their White colleagues and have to work harder to get the same recognition. Moreover, they must walk the tightrope of being expected to work on company culture and inclusion while being penalized for diversity-promoting behavior. Don't add to that pressure.

Remember, as important as your conversation with your boss is, action is really where the rubber meets the road. To be an effective antiracist, you have to do more than just talk—you have to take action. That action doesn't have to be earth-shattering. In fact, it may feel quite small. But small, consistent, progressive action over time can result in dramatic change.

Give it a shot. See what happens.

9

AND . . . KEEP STEPPING
WHEN YOU SHOULD MOVE ON

When I look back at my career, some of my biggest regrets are over staying too long in situations that no longer suited me. Sometimes it was because of financial necessity. Those student loans don't pay themselves off, and my parents made government salaries. I was also afraid—that I couldn't do better, that the next place would be worse than the last. My fear kept me stuck. And it never worked out. Each time I stayed too long, it ended badly anyway.

Sometimes it's better to just walk away. Of course, we don't all have the privilege to do that, particularly if we're from marginalized groups. We may not have the financial security, or we might have extended family depending on us for financial support. And we may not all be given the benefit of the doubt if we've left our prior roles under less than favorable circumstances, without glowing references. Even if we have more privilege, walking away can be difficult. It may feel like we're abandoning our colleagues or foregoing a once-in-a-lifetime opportunity.

But sometimes walking away is the only answer. No matter what your personal situation is, I humbly suggest that if you are in a situation so toxic it can't be redeemed, when it comes to finding a new role, the question should be how, not if. Think about the goals that you have for yourself. Now, take a close look at the behavioral patterns you're following and your physical and emotional well-being. If you don't see a path to where you want to be from where you are now, it is time to go.

If it makes you feel any better, you wouldn't be alone. Before the pandemic, one in five Americans left their jobs because of toxicity in the workplace. That turnover cost employers nearly $222 billion over the course of five years. After the pandemic, turnover got worse, as the United

States entered what we are now calling the Great Resignation. As of June 2021, more than 95 percent of workers considered leaving their jobs, as workers reevaluated the kind of treatment they were willing to accept.

Yes, there's always a chance that you'll be replaced by someone who proudly wears the red cap and wants to leave politics at the door. But your departure could also be the wake-up call your bosses need.

Some of the most high-profile wins against problematic organizations have come as a result of public departures. Susan Fowler's blog post blowing the whistle on sexual harassment at Uber led to an investigation that got the CEO of her company fired. Ifeoma Ozoma filed race and gender claims against her former employer, Pinterest, and won a settlement that led to the effort to introduce the Silenced No More Act in California. This legislation would prohibit overly expansive NDAs from covering up any form of discrimination or harassment.

Of course, like the other tactics we've explored in this book, there is an art to leaving. Throwing deuces and quitting on the spot may sound satisfying, but that feeling of pleasure quickly fades when the rent comes due, that unemployment check is nowhere to be found, and the former colleagues you had good relationships with are too busy cleaning up the mess you left behind to serve as references. Don't let it get to the point where you explode and do something you regret. Give yourself enough time to set yourself up for the outcome that you want and preserve the relationships worth saving.

WARNING SIGNS

We'll get to the how in a second. But I would argue that more important than that is the when.

Many of us want to believe the best—in our colleagues, in our departments, and in our organizations. So we miss the neon warning signs practically screaming at us to leave. In the best-case scenario, we spend longer at a crappy job than necessary. But the worst-case scenario is that by missing these warning signs, we give the racists time to see us as a threat and undermine our careers.

What follows are a few ways to tell that your organization may not be ready to change.

RETALIATION

Let's say you have a conversation with your boss or engage in other antiracism work. Then, you find you're experiencing a mysterious uptick in constructive criticism of your work, unjustifiably worse performance reviews, and more frequent conversations with HR. That's retaliation.

We talked about this extensively in the chapter on backlash, but it merits a mention here too. In all likelihood, you may experience some form of retaliation for your advocacy. Eventually, you will need to figure out if it is serious enough to make you leave.

It's important to come to terms with the fact that folks are likely maneuvering to sideline you or push you out altogether. As we've noted earlier, you should keep thorough records and explore your legal options. It's a good idea to consider the option of transferring out of your department or leaving your organization altogether. It depends on what you want. If you want justice, maybe stay and fight. If you just want to do your work in peace (nothing wrong with that), it's probably time to move on.

INCOMPLETE INITIATIVES

If your organization talks a big game but has a hard time following through, that could also be a sign to go. In my experience, failure to act on DEI promises is due to either a lack of experience and expertise or a lack of commitment. You are in a position to solve the former problem, but the latter can be career quicksand. If your organization has failed to bring on an expert in DEI or is still struggling to get buy-in at the highest levels even after some time has passed, it may be time to come to terms with the fact that they are probably all talk—in which case, they aren't ever going to be able to come through with the progress you are looking for. If you need that progress to stay motivated, or even just to do your job well and without interference, your current job probably isn't the right one for you.

LACK OF DEVOTED RESOURCES

Relatedly, if your organization never seems to have the resources to devote to fighting racism—if your ERGs are underfunded, if your company can't afford to hire experts, if everyone is working off the side of their desk and no one has a budget—then that may be a sign that you're in for trouble. If your organization "really cares" about racism only up to the point where they have to pay actual money to solve it, then they don't really care. Organizations show what they value by spending money on those things. Sure, it takes time to get the ball rolling at an organization just getting started on its antiracism journey. You may want to wait a quarter or two before you start to read the room. But if you have been working on a shoestring DEI budget for longer than six months, you might need to think about whether or not your company really cares, and whether this pace will be good for you in the long run.

Organizations that don't value diversity but want to look like they do are happy to let you run yourself ragged inching your way toward progress. They don't mind if you exhaust yourself or burn out on DEI work. Arguably, that's the point: give the employees just enough to placate them and exhaust them so that the organization doesn't have to actually change. Make no mistake, Sisyphus, there is no mountaintop here. You're just going to keep arduously trying to push that boulder up that hill until it rolls back and crushes you or you collapse of exhaustion.

THINGS GET WORSE

Maybe it doesn't amount to full-blown retaliation, and it might not even be directed at you, but it could be that after you start the work of antiracism you notice some *pushback*. Maybe the problematic jokes become more common, or you notice more frequent microaggressions. Perhaps people start talking about focusing on the work instead of "politics." As we've discussed, you should anticipate some friction or pushback when you ask people to wrestle with racism. But if the manifestations of fragility are protracted and get worse over time, it may not be worth it to dig in your heels, especially if there is no accountability for the bad behavior.

THINGS TO KNOW BEFORE YOU GO

You've seen the warning signs and decided to leave. But how do you make it count? Sometimes, your exit strategy can be as simple as: Find a new job, give notice, bide my two weeks, don't burn any bridges, and peace out. But it could also be more complicated. Leaving can send a powerful signal to your company and draw attention to racism and bad behavior. Maybe you're in a position to leave with a bang, and a press release is in order. As you decide your exit strategy, keep the following tips in mind:

FIGURE OUT THE OUTCOME YOU WANT

Do you want to blow the whistle and create a public relations nightmare for your organization? Do you want your day in court, or do you just want a new job at a better place? Each of these outcomes requires a slightly different approach. If you're going to go public, make sure you have a compelling narrative, tight messaging, and someone interested in telling your story. If you just want another job, do what you can to maintain the relationships that are good and start looking for other roles as soon as you get the indication that your current job might not work out. Whatever the goal, make sure that your exit strategy supports it, and get help along the way. Bounce ideas off your mentors, especially if they work for a different company. Lean on your network for job leads, help writing a statement, or references. Work with a therapist to manage your emotions in the interim.

MAKE SURE QUITTING IS REALLY THE SOLUTION

Ask yourself: Is this an organizational problem, or a problem limited to my specific department? It could be that you don't need to bail. While some cultural elements persist across organizations, there are those companies where culture, demographic diversity, standards of behavior, and values differ significantly from team to team or office to office. If all you want is to work in peace and your organization as a whole isn't that bad, maybe an internal transfer will work just as well for you. If you're open to it and your organization has the infrastructure for you to do so, explore opportunities on other teams. It could be delaying the inevitable, but a transfer might just give you the breathing room you need to make it work.

GIVE NOTICE EARLY, BUT NOT TOO EARLY

Two weeks is the standard, but your boss may ask you to work longer or train your replacement. If you can stand to do so then by all means, stay to make the transition as smooth as possible. But be aware that if your workplace is toxic enough to make you quit, it's also very likely that it's toxic enough to make the weeks leading up to your departure a living hell. So time your notice carefully. Then again, they may ask you to leave as soon as you tell them, and that will be that. Either way, make sure you have everything ready to go in case you have to leave in a hurry. To the extent that you can do so without violating your company's data security policies, make sure that you have a copy of your contacts, personal photos (digital or physical), other personal items in your office if you work in person, and anything personal you may have saved on your computer or phone. Get your affairs in order and a written offer for a new job in hand before breaking the news.

UNDERSTAND YOUR NONDISCLOSURE AGREEMENT

Nearly one third of the American workforce is bound by nondisclosure agreements, contractual obligations often included in employment contracts or settlement agreements that restrict or outright prohibit employees from discussing workplace matters. The #MeToo movement drew attention to how NDAs have been used to silence employees facing discrimination. Since then, more than twenty-six states have introduced legislation restricting the use of NDAs in cases of sexual harassment, sexual violence, or discrimination. Now we're seeing a similar push in regard to racial discrimination. The aforementioned Silenced No More Act is just one example.

Not that I would ever advise you to break the law, but if you were to break an NDA, it's not exactly certain there would be repercussions. Zelda Perkins, a former employee of Miramax in London, broke her NDA to shed light on the system that protected Harvey Weinstein and has not faced legal punishment. So if you signed an NDA be sure to review it and, if you can afford it, ask an expert on employment law in your state about your rights, especially if you plan on blowing the whistle. If cost is an issue, research legal clinics in your area that may be able to help you for a reduced cost. You may have more room to maneuver than you think.

EMBRACE YOUR NARRATIVE

Get your story straight, because people will ask. Expect questions from inquisitive colleagues, interviewers for new jobs, or investigators. You may even need or want to post publicly on the internet about your departure. This is not an encouragement to lie. Lying is a great way to trash your credibility and undermine the very real cultural issues your colleagues may still have to face. Instead, I'm encouraging you to get comfortable telling your own story.

First, know your facts. If you've been documenting issues all along, great. Review that documentation and consider how much of your experience and the experiences of others you want to share (with their consent and respecting their confidentiality). Then, think about the way you want to frame your departure and consider your audience. What you share with colleagues with whom you don't want to burn bridges may be different from what you share with a state labor board to whom you file a complaint.

Finally, consider your tone. I know, I know. I'm not trying to tone police you. That said, depending on your identity and the audience you want to reach, cool, clinical, and detached may go a lot further than hurt and horrified. Susan Fowler's three-thousand-word blog post about the toxic, sexist culture at Uber is simply titled "Reflecting on One Very, Very Strange Year at Uber." The dispassionate, detached way she lays out the litany of sexist abuse that she faced resonated with readers and journalists alike, from Kara Swisher at Recode to the *New York Times*. Of course, there are aspects to her story that gave it more traction: Fowler faced gender-based harassment (more likely to resonate with White readers) and she is a conventionally attractive, young White woman (same). But it still demonstrates that there are a range of ways to tell your story that will resonate with and move the people whom you want to reach.

GET EMOTIONAL AND MENTAL HEALTH SUPPORT

You don't want to bring the trauma from your last job to your next one. Work-related, race-based trauma is still trauma. The last organization I worked for before I started my own company (frankly, it was the reason why I started my own company) was by far the most toxic I've ever experienced. The abuse was textbook. I was gaslit, berated, manipulated, excluded, and passed over for promotion by a White boss with anger issues who was supported by my White colleagues. I was messed up for a long time after I left. That experience shook my self-confidence and impacted my ability to trust others. I wish I'd had help in working through the trauma inflicted on me.

I know I'm not alone. Sadly, I see every day in my work that people bring their trauma with them. It's not their fault. We've been taught to expect toxicity and trained to believe that if you let it get to you, you are weak. There could be nothing further from the truth. Being emotionally affected by trauma doesn't make you weak; it makes you human. Getting help for that trauma (if you are privileged enough to have access to it) so that you can better take care of yourself and build relationships with others is a sign of strength and maturity.

Even if you haven't experienced trauma, letting go from a relationship as closely tied to your identity as work often is, can still be tough. Make sure you put supportive structures, like a good network of friends, in place to help you move on.

IF YOU GET FIRED

Unfortunately, you may not have control over when you leave an organization. They may just fire you. If that happens, remember the following:

Don't feel ashamed. Organizations that push people out want those people to think that it's their fault. They want you to feel shame. Shame keeps you quiet. Shame makes you sign legally binding documents you normally wouldn't. But you have nothing to be ashamed of. The truth is that lots of people who try to change their organizations for the better—or, heck, even strive just to be treated as an equal—get pushed out. Some of the people you most admire have been fired. I was fired from that aforementioned shitty, toxic organization before starting my company, and it was the best thing that could have happened to me. It forced me to leave an organization where I would never thrive and create the place where I could. Don't let your former employer shame you into keeping quiet and doing something that doesn't serve you. Which leads to my next point...

Don't sign anything before consulting with an attorney. As I recommended when discussing how to deal with backlash, you should seek legal counsel. A lawyer can tell you whether the NDA that you are about to sign in exchange for severance is actually legal, if you may be entitled to more compensation, or if your former employer may be trying to prevent you from receiving benefits.

Negotiate your exit. Believe it or not, you still have some power here, especially if your employer is trying to sweep some bad behavior under the rug. Just as you negotiated your job offer, negotiate your exit. The amount of your severance, whether or not you get a reference, and whether you have to sign an NDA are all negotiable. Now in my experience, companies hate when you do this. It could backfire. But at this point, you don't have a lot to lose. Definitely bring in a lawyer to keep it from getting too personal too quickly, and be prepared for some brinkmanship.

No matter how your exit happens, don't feel guilty about it. Employers want us to believe our jobs are our identity and how we prove our worth. That's how they keep people working in conditions that aren't good for them. In reality, jobs are jobs. Employers hire you and compensate you to work. You are doing them a favor (and extra labor) if you also help them see how they might improve their culture, attract a more diverse pool of talent, and leverage that diversity to improve their business. They don't also get to take your health and emotional well-being on top of that.

CONCLUSION

TAKE CARE OF YOURSELF

More and more, this book reminds me of a dying star.

By the time you read these words, the world they were written in will be gone.

As I speak to you, reading this sometime in the future, I hope with my whole heart that things have gotten better.

I signed the contract for this book in the middle of a pandemic. I was seven months pregnant, terrified to give birth in a country that all too often let mothers like me die. I started writing it as violent protests exploded on the streets. In some cities, police were happy to gas protestors for having the audacity to claim my life mattered.

My dad was diagnosed with stage 4 lymphoma around chapter 2. My beautiful daughter was born shortly after. My body started to heal around chapter 4. We left our home in the Bay Area around chapter 5, when the fires made it too difficult for me, an asthmatic, and my daughter, a newborn, to breathe.

My big sister died somewhere in the middle of chapter 7. She was the one who took care of my dad when he got sick. The one who said, "Don't worry, I got it. You have a company to run, a child to raise, and a book to write." I didn't get a chance to really thank her for that.

White supremacists breached the Capitol Building and attempted a coup in chapter 8. Trump was acquitted of impeachment toward the end of chapter 9, right around the time people finally started to pay attention to a dramatic rise in anti-Asian violence. In the days before I handed this manuscript to my editor, that violence resulted in the tragic killing spree targeting Asian women in Atlanta.

Strange, traumatizing times we live in. Typical times too.

I spent quite a bit of this book talking to White people. That's because I believe that the burden of addressing racism can't just fall to people of color, as it has for so long. If we're going to dismantle racism, White people, the ones with privilege, must play an active role in dismantling it.

The reality is that quite often, we people of color are the first people called on to have difficult conversations about race. We're the ones relied on to offer solutions to solve racism inside of problematic organizations. That ask is fraught with risk. Given the ways that our communities have been devastated by COVID-19, the fact that we've lost a disproportionate number of jobs and have been targeted for violence, the consequences of speaking out are as dire as ever. And many of us desperately need time to heal.

Regardless of your racial identity, you, dear reader, are likely reading this book, encountering this time capsule, with some hurt of your own. If you've read this far, you also harbor the desire to make sure that all we've been through leads to something better.

I commend you for that. I really do.

Just one thing. One really quick thing. Make sure you take care of yourself along the way.

We've already discussed some self-care strategies in this book, like knowing when to leave a truly toxic environment and making sure you have emotional support. But I have more to say.

After I lost my sister, I got really scared I was going to lose myself. I felt like I had exhausted all of my reserves. Between the pandemic, work, the baby, the book, and the social unrest, I had nothing left. Actually, I was operating at a deficit, and I knew it was only a matter of time before something went really wrong. So I got help. I worked with someone to help me set better personal and professional boundaries and support me as I processed my grief. Today, my self-care routine involves long walks with my dog, short daily meditation sessions, and regular therapy.

That's what works for me. You should find what works for you. But there are some crucial things we should all remember:

Don't work two jobs at once uncompensated. If, after your conversation, you're asked to lead or even participate more actively in the antiracism work in your organization, take on the additional responsibility with caution. Working more for the same amount of money and limited recognition is a recipe for burnout. Carve out diversity and antiracism work as part of your role. During your performance review, make sure you get paid to do it and that it is considered as part of your job. If someone asks you to lead an ERG or DEI committee, have these conversations and align expectations early.

Learn how to say no. You know the book *If You Give a Mouse a Cookie*? It's about a boy who gives a mouse a cookie, and then that mouse keeps asking the kid for more stuff, until ultimately (spoiler alert) the mouse asks for another cookie, and the cycle starts all over again. That's often what culture work inside of a company looks like, especially if it's being done for free. People will ask you to put on events, they'll want to pull you aside to pick your brain, heck, they may even push you to create an entire strategy, all in addition to the work that you are already doing. It can be hard to say no.

Racism is personal. It deeply affects our lives and/or the lives of people we love and respect. It offends our sense of justice. Whether we like it or not, no matter who we are, we are affected by racism in some way—by the benefits it confers, by the challenges it places in front of us, by its impact on the society in which we live. It can be hard to set boundaries, take a step back, or say no when the work has to be done. We feel guilty when we do.

But we can't do it all. You becoming a martyr for some company's slapped-together antiracism push isn't going to get you to the mountaintop. Saying no isn't failure. Saying no is permission to rest, replenish ourselves, and live to fight another day. Be honest with yourself about how much you can and can't do. Then give yourself permission not to participate. That doesn't mean you care about fighting racism any less. It just means that you care about taking care of yourself too.

Take it to the group chat. I'm part of several group chats made up of other professional women of color where I get to vent about the things I have sense enough not to share on Twitter. (Shout out PI, shout out #squad.) It's not all heavy stuff; we also trade memes, jokes, pictures of baby animals, and professional tips. The women in those group chats also gave me encouragement when I was down and hyped me up for my victories (no matter how small I tell myself they are). Without them, the work that I do would feel really lonely. And as I have said so many times in this book, you can't do this work alone.

Seek out or create a supportive professional network. Find people who you can learn from and grow with. Beyond emotional support, a robust professional network can provide you better access to opportunities (in case you do need a new job), information (in case you want to negotiate a better salary), and resources (like other professional connections). Particularly if you are a person of color, this kind of community can be invaluable.

More important, don't forget about your relationships with your family and friends. I never thought I would be one of those people who would say that her mom is one of her best friends, yet here we are. Trust and believe that I had to do a lot of work to get our relationship to this point. Now we can chat on the phone for hours. I'm always struck by how many of the things I experience as a Black woman that she's also seen.

She still surprises me. Last summer, we were talking about the Black Lives Matter protests and what they could mean. She casually dropped the fact that she marched with Martin Luther King Jr. and hid out during the 1968 riots in Detroit. "Girl, this ain't nothing new," she said. "I remember when they was throwing bricks in Detroit." Readers, she said it like it was nothing. Like she was talking about having a night out or the latest celebrity scandal and not one of the most significant and deadliest Black uprisings in American history.

Girl, this ain't nothing new, indeed.

Only a Black mother could provide that kind of perspective. I know that not everyone is able to connect in a healthy way with their biological family, but you can also reach out to your chosen family. Tend to those relationships. They will be there for you long after your job is gone, in a way that your employer could never be. *Family* is family, not your workplace.

Log off. When your work is antiracism, it can be tempting to invest heavily in your presence online to stay plugged in to critical conversations, build community, continue your learning, and raise awareness. But being online offers diminishing returns. At some point, you need to log off. It's important to know when to close your laptop or put down your phone and walk outside or read a book or get a snack.

First, we all experience harm when exposed to too

much social media. Extensive use of social media has been tied to depression, lowered self-esteem, anxiety, and sleeplessness.

But doomscrolling can be particularly pernicious for people of color. Online exposure to images of tragic racist events such as the murder of George Floyd is more likely to cause depression and trigger PTSD in viewers of color, for whom the racism they experience every day is compounded by the vicarious trauma of seeing an innocent person who looks like them and shares that same experience die on film.

Finally, people of color, particularly women and nonbinary people, are more targeted for abuse and harassment online—doubly so if they are actively involved in discussions about racism.

So watch how much time you spend online and what content you consume. Staying informed is good. Getting absorbed, not so much.

Therapy is your friend. If you can afford it and have access, please, for the love of God, go get therapy. Go get it before you think you need it. There doesn't have to be anything "wrong" with you for you to benefit from talking to someone, especially if you find yourself frequently engaging in the emotional labor often associated with antiracist work.

Nowadays there are also great alternatives to traditional therapy that make getting access to a therapist much easier. I use an online platform for therapy. It gave me greater flexibility and a broader range of therapists. I wanted to work with a Black woman who shared and understood my social identity. Going the virtual route made it so much easier to find that person, given how few Black women therapists there are—just 4 percent of therapists in the US are Black.

If cost is an issue, there may be organizations that can help you. The Boris Lawrence Henson Foundation, National Queer and Trans Therapists of Color Network, the Loveland Foundation, and Real to the People all offer financial support for therapy or free therapy sessions for Black people or people of color. If you aren't a person of color, try a resource like Open Path Psychotherapy Collective, a membership network that offers affordable therapy sessions.

Remember that you are more than your job. In the United States, it's customary to ask someone upon meeting them, "What do you do?" We've been taught to look to work to help define our identity and our sense of self-worth. For many of us, work isn't just about economic production, it's about fulfilling our purpose or living up to our potential. Landing our dream job is the ultimate success and the culmination of a life of hard work and sacrifice (and maybe a ginormous mountain of student loan debt).

This is even more true if you come from a background where people who look like you haven't always had the chance to have dream jobs. It can be all the more crushing when the dream job turns into a toxic-working-environment nightmare and you fear that you have nowhere else to go. In so many ways, the rejection that you experience on the job can feel like a rejection of you as a human being and a repudiation of all that potential you thought you had. That, more than just stress or burnout, I believe is associated with so much of the trauma that comes from experiencing racism at work.

You are so much more than your work and your hustle. You are a full human being whose value is rooted in so much more than your economic contribution. What you create, the lives you change, the way you love: that's what matters. When all of this is said and done, that is the legacy you will leave behind.

Cultivate an identity outside of work. Make sure that fulfilling your purpose means more to you than simply working harder. If fighting racism is part of that purpose, explore the ways that you can do that outside of the workplace too.

GODSPEED, DEAR FRIEND

You know, if I could give you a hug, I would. You've chosen quite the battle to fight. While we've won a few skirmishes here and there, we've yet to come out on the other side.

But as the saying goes: If we aren't all free, none of us are free.

If we aren't all able to live up to our full potential, none of us are.

Earlier in this book, I gave you a list of the things I lost in the fight to be treated like a full human being. It hurt to write it.

But then I imagined what I would have lost if I stayed silent. I would have lost myself, my dignity, my faith in others. That would have hurt a lot more.

I didn't ask to be born Black. You didn't ask to be born White or Asian or Latinx or Native or Pacific Islander or some combination of all of the above. We didn't ask for our historical inheritance.

But here we are. We have it.

The question now is, what do we do with it? We can choose the legacy we leave behind.

I hope that this book empowers you to leave your job (your family, your friend group, the world) a little bit better for others than you found it. I hope that you are able to give someone a chance who might not have had one otherwise. I hope, collectively, we fuck up the playing field (even if it's just a little bit). I hope all the while, you find joy.

Okay, I'll let you go (for now). We've got a lot of work to do. It starts with a conversation.

Godspeed.

NOTES

PREFACE

xx **increased only by a few hundred thousand workers:** Annie Lowrey, "Workers Should Have the Power to Say 'No': Policy Makers Should Not Ensure a Flood of Low-wage Workers for America's Businesses," *The Atlantic*, June 1, 2021, https://www.theatlantic.com/ideas/archive/2021/06/labor-shortage-positive/619050/.

CHAPTER 1

2   **Consider the words of Dr. Martin Luther King Jr:** Dr. Martin Luther King Jr., "Remaining Awake Through a Great Revolution," commencement address given at Oberlin College, Oberlin, OH, June 1965, https://www2.oberlin.edu/external/EOG/BlackHistoryMonth/MLK/CommAddress.html.

6   **"a power construct of blended difference that lives socially":** Ibram X. Kendi, *How to Be an Antiracist* (New York: One World, 2019), 38.

7   **race is a poor marker for the relationship:** Michael Yudell, Dorothy Roberts, Rob DeSalle, and Sarah Tishkoff, "Taking Race Out of Human Genetics," *Science* 351, no. 6273 (February 2016): 564–65, https://doi.org/10.1126/science.aac4951.

8 "Latinx" is not used as widely: Luis Noe-Bustamante, Lauren Mora, and Mark Hugo Lopez, "About One-in-Four U.S. Hispanics Have Heard of Latinx, but Just 3% Use It: Young Hispanic Women Among the Most Likely to Use the Term," Pew Research Center report, August 11, 2020, https://www.pewresearch.org/hispanic /2020/08/11/about-one-in-four-u-s-hispanics-have-heard-of-latinx -but-just-3-use-it/.

10 reinforced by systems of power: Paula Rothenberg and Christina Hsu Accomando, *Race, Class, and Gender in the United States: An Integrated Study*, 11th ed. (New York: Worth Publishers/Macmillan Learning), 127.

13 engage in racial gaslighting: Natalie Morris, "What Is 'Racial Gaslighting'—and Why Is It So Damaging for People of Colour?" *Metro*, June 18, 2020, https://metro.co.uk/2020/06/18/what-racial -gaslighting-why-damaging-people-colour-12866409/.

14 your experiences were actually the result of racism: Angelique M. Davis and Rose Ernst, "Racial Gaslighting," *Politics, Groups, and Identities* 7, no. 4 (2019): 761–74, https://doi.org/10.1080/2156 5503.2017.1403934.

16 coined by Harvard psychiatrist Dr. Chester M. Pierce: Chester Pierce, "Psychiatric Problems of the Black Minority," in Silvano Arieti, ed., *American Handbook of Psychiatry* (New York: Basic Books, 1974), 512–23.

16 popularized by Dr. Derald Wing Sue: Derald Wing Sue et al., "Racial Microaggressions in Everyday Life: Implications for Clinical Practice," *American Psychologist* 62, no. 4 (May–June 2007): 271–86, https://www.cpedv.org/sites/main/files/file-attachments/how _to_be_an_effective_ally-lessons_learned_microaggressions.pdf.

18 Racial microaggressions have been linked: Victoria M. O'Keefe, LaRicka R. Wingate, Ashley B. Cole, David W. Hollingsworth, and Raymond P. Tucker, "Seemingly Harmless Racial Communications Are Not So Harmless: Racial Microaggressions Lead to Suicidal Ideation by Way of Depression Symptoms," *Suicide and Life-Threatening Behavior* 45, no. 5 (October 2015): 567–76, https://doi .org/10.1111/sltb.12150.

18 elevated risk of heart disease: Derald Wing Sue, *Microaggressions in Everyday Life: Race, Gender, and Sexual Orientation* (Hoboken, NJ: Wiley, 2010), 97.

21 work together to create and reinforce racism: Kwame Ture and Charles V. Hamilton, *Black Power: The Politics of Liberation in America* (New York: Vintage Books, 1992); Eduardo Bonilla-Silva, "Rethinking Racism: Toward a Structural Interpretation," *American Sociological Review* 62, no. 3 (June 1997): 465–80, https://doi .org/10.2307/2657316; John A. Powell, "Structural Racism: Building upon the Insights of John Calmore," *North Carolina Law Review* 86, no. 3 (March 2008): 791–816, https://scholarship.law.unc.edu/nclr /vol86/iss3/8/; William M. Wiececk and Judy L. Hamilton, "Beyond the Civil Rights Act of 1964: Confronting Structural Racism in the Workplace," *Louisiana Law Review* 74, no. 4 (Summer 2014): 1095– 1160, https://digitalcommons.law.lsu.edu/lalrev/vol74/iss4/5.

21 regardless of individual action or intent: Powell, "Structural Racism"; Gilbert C. Gee and Chandra L. Ford, "Structural Racism and Health Inequities: Old Issues, New Directions," *Du Bois Review: Social Science Research on Race* 8, no. 1 (2011): 115–32, doi:10.1017 /S1742058X11000130.

22 worse outcomes for marginalized people of color: Powell, "Structural Racism."

24 Law professor Kimberlé Crenshaw coined the term: Kimberlé Crenshaw, "Demarginalizing the Intersection of Race and Sex: A Black Feminist Critique of Antidiscrimination Doctrine, Feminist Theory and Antiracist Politics," *University of Chicago Legal Forum* 1989, Article 8, https://chicagounbound.uchicago.edu/uclf/vol1989/iss1 /8. The foundations of intersectionality can also be found in Combahee River Collective, "The Combahee River Collective Statement," in Zillah Eisenstein, ed., *Capitalist Patriarchy and the Case for Socialist Feminism* (New York: Monthly Review Press, 1979), 362–72, http://circuitous.org/scraps/combahee.html.

25 primary beneficiaries of affirmative action: Victoria M. Massie, "White Women Benefit Most from Affirmative Action—and Are Among Its Fiercest Opponents," *Vox*, June 23, 2016, https://www

.vox.com/2016/5/25/11682950/fisher-supreme-court-white-women -affirmative-action.

25 more often than their White female peers: Zuhairah Washington and Laura Morgan Roberts, "Women of Color Get Less Support at Work. Here's How Managers Can Changes That," *Harvard Business Review*, March 4, 2019, https://hbr.org/2019/03/women-of-color -get-less-support-at-work-heres-how-managers-can-change-that.

25 for asserting herself in the workplace: Joan C. Williams, "Double Jeopardy? An Empirical Study with Implications for the Debates over Implicit Bias and Intersectionality," *Harvard Journal of Law and Gender 37* (2014): 185–242, http://repository.uchastings.edu /faculty_scholarship/1278.

28 antiracism has deep historical roots: Gargi Bhattacharyya, Satnam Virdee, and Aaron Winter, "Revisiting Histories of Anti-Racist Thought and Activism," *Identities: Global Studies in Culture and Power* 27, no. 1 (2020): 1–19, https://doi.org/10.1080/1070289X.2019 .1647686.

29 blame Black people for their condition: Ibram X. Kendi, *Stamped from the Beginning: The Definitive History of Racist Ideas in America* (New York: Bold Type Books, 2017), 2.

30 "The claim of 'not racist' neutrality is a mask for racism": Kendi, *How to Be an Antiracist*, 8.

31 hasn't improved for African Americans since 1990: Lincoln Quillian, Devah Pager, Ole Hexel, and Arnfinn H. Midtbøen, "Meta-analysis of Field Experiments Shows No Change in Racial Discrimination in Hiring Over Time," *Proceedings of the National Academy of Sciences* 114, no. 41 (October 10, 2017): 10870–75, https://doi.org/10.1073/pnas.1706255114.

31 than résumés with Black sounding names: Marianne Bertrand and Sendhil Mullainathan, "Are Emily and Greg More Employable than Lakisha and Jamal? A Field Experiment on Labor Market Discrimination," National Bureau of Economic Research Working Paper 9873, July 2003, https://doi.org/10.3386/w9873.

31 Black men faced worse hiring discrimination: Rebecca Beitsch, "'Ban the Box' Laws May Be Harming Young Black Men Seeking

Jobs," *Stateline* (blog), Pew Charitable Trusts, August 22, 2017, https://www.pewtrusts.org/en/research-and-analysis/blogs/state line/2017/08/22/ban-the-box-laws-may-be-harming-young-black -men-seeking-jobs.

31 assumed that Black men had criminal records: Beitsch, "'Ban the Box' Laws."

31– 32 They are overrepresented in low-paying jobs: Kelemwork Cook et al., "The Future of Work in Black America," McKinsey & Company, October 4, 2019, https://www.mckinsey.com/featured-insights/future -of-work/the-future-of-work-in-black-america#.

32 share of the population and their qualifications: Michael Gee, "Why Aren't Black Employees Getting More White-Collar Jobs?" *Harvard Business Review*, February 28, 2018, https://hbr.org/2018/02/why -arent-black-employees-getting-more-white-collar-jobs.

32 unemployed at twice the rate of White workers: Sarah Rawlins and Nicolas Buffie, "The Different Experiences of Black Unemployment and White Unemployment," Center for Economic Policy and Research, March 30, 2017, https://cepr.net/the-different-experiences -of-black-unemployment-and-white-unemployment/.

32 African Americans make up 13 percent: US Bureau of Labor Statistics, "Labor Force Characteristics by Race and Ethnicity, 2018," BLS Reports, Report 1082, October 2019, https://www.bls.gov /opub/reports/race-and-ethnicity/2018/home.htm.

32 hovers between 5 and 7 percent: Bourree Lam, "The Least Diverse Jobs in America," *The Atlantic*, June 29, 2015, https://www.the atlantic.com/business/archive/2015/06/diversity-jobs-professions -america/396632/.

33 Google's leadership is 2.6 percent Black and 3.7 percent Latinx: Rob Copeland, "Google Sets Hiring Goal to Advance Black Executives," *Wall Street Journal*, June 17, 2020, https://www.wsj.com /articles/google-adds-new-hiring-goal-to-boost-black-executives -11592421504.

33 Fewer than 20 percent of studio executives: Dr. Darnell Hunt and Dr. Ana-Christina Ramón, *Hollywood Diversity Report 2020: A Tale of Two Hollywoods: Part 1: Film* (Los Angeles: UCLA College of

Social Sciences, Institute for Research on Labor and Employment, 2020), https://socialsciences.ucla.edu/wp-content/uploads/2020/02/UCLA-Hollywood-Diversity-Report-2020-Film-2-6-2020.pdf.

33 **2 percent of law firm partners are Black:** Orlando R. Richmond Sr., "A Black Partner's Perspective on Why Law Firms Are Failing at Diversity," *Fortune,* June 11, 2020, https://fortune.com/2020/06/11/law-firms-black-diversity-inclusion/.

33–34 **only 10 percent:** Subodh Mishra, "U.S. Board Diversity Trends in 2019," Harvard Law School Forum on Corporate Governance, June 18, 2019, https://corpgov.law.harvard.edu/2019/06/18/u-s-board-diversity-trends-in-2019/.

34 **154 percent more likely to hold executive roles:** "The Leadership Representation Ceiling for Asian Americans," Bloomberg, May 27, 2020, https://www.bloomberg.com/company/stories/the-leadership-representation-ceiling-for-asian-americans/.

35 **little to no impact on performance:** Thomas Koulopoulos, "Performance Reviews Are Dead: Here's What You Should Do Instead," *Inc.*, February 25, 2018, https://www.inc.com/thomas-koulopoulos/performance-reviews-are-dead-heres-what-you-should-do-instead.html.

35 **particularly fraught for employees of color:** Jeffrey H. Greenhaus, Saroj Parasuraman, and Wayne M. Wormley, "Effects of Race on Organizational Experiences, Job Performance Evaluations, and Career Outcomes," *The Academy of Management Journal* 33, no. 1 (1990): 64–86, https://doi.org/10.2307/256352; Beth Jones, Khalil Smith, and David Rock, "3 Biases that Hijack Performance Reviews, and How to Address Them," *Harvard Business Review*, June 20, 2018, https://hbr.org/2018/06/3-biases-that-hijack-performance-reviews-and-how-to-address-them; Joseph M. Stauffer and M. Ronald Buckley, "The Existence and Nature of Racial Bias in Supervisory Ratings," *Journal of Applied Psychology* 90, no. 3 (2005): 586–91, https://doi.org/ 10.1037/0021-9010.90.3.586.

36 **success in marginalized groups is attributed to luck:** Jennifer L. Knight, Michelle R. Hebl, Jessica B. Foster, and Laura M. Mannix, "Out of Role? Out of Luck: The Influence of Race and Leadership

Status on Performance Appraisals," *Journal of Leadership and Organizational Studies* 9, no. 3 (August 2003): 85–93, https://doi.org/10.1177/107179190300900308.

36 there's even more room for bias to creep in: Lori Nishiura Mackenzie, JoAnne Wehner, and Shelley J. Correll, "Why Most Performance Evaluations Are Biased, and How to Fix Them," *Harvard Business Review,* January 11, 2019, https://hbr.org/2019/01/why-most-performance-evaluations-are-biased-and-how-to-fix-them.

36 when their manager is the same race as them: Laura Giuliano, David I. Levine, and Jonathan Leonard, "Racial Bias in the Manager-Employee Relationship: An Analysis of Quits, Dismissals, and Promotions at a Large Retail Firm," *Journal of Human Resources* 46, no. 1 (Winter 2011): 26–52, https://doi.org/10.1353/jhr.2011.0022.

37 White women, who make up 29 percent: Rachel Thomas et al., *Women in the Workplace: 2019,* Lean In and McKinsey & Company, https://womenintheworkplace.com/2019.

37 dissatisfaction with a manager who is a person of color: Giuliano, Levine, and Leonard, "Racial Bias in the Manager-Employee Relationship."

39 similarly qualified White counterparts: Sarah Myers West, Meredith Whittaker, and Kate Crawford, *Discriminating Systems: Gender, Race and Power in AI,* AI Now Institute (New York: New York University, April 2019), https://ainowinstitute.org/discriminatingsystems.html.

39 penalized for negotiating their salaries: Morela Hernandez, Derek R. Avery, Sabrina D. Volpone, and Cheryl R. Kaiser, "Bargaining While Black: The Role of Race in Salary Negotiations," *Journal of Applied Psychology* 104, no. 4 (2018): 581–92.

40 work that leads to accolades and promotions: Joan C. Williams and Marina Multhaup, "For Women and Minorities to Get Ahead, Managers Must Assign Work Fairly," *Harvard Business Review*, March 5, 2018, https://hbr.org/2018/03/for-women-and-minorities-to-get-ahead-managers-must-assign-work-fairly.

41 penalized for not conforming: Jennifer L. Berdahl and Ji-A Min, "Prescriptive Stereotypes and Workplace Consequences for East Asians in North America," *Cultural Diversity and Ethnic Minority*

Psychology 18, no. 2 (April 2012): 141–52, https://doi.org/10.1037 /a0027692.

42 departments that fail to hold racists accountable: Sarah Jensen Clayton, "6 Signs Your Corporate Culture is a Liability," *Harvard Business Review*, December 5, 2019, https://hbr.org/2019/12/6-signs -your-corporate-culture-is-a-liability.

43 both quit toxic organizations: Jonathan S. Leonard and David I. Levine, "The Effect of Diversity on Turnover: A Large Case Study," *ILR Journal* 59, no. 4 (July 2006): 542–72, https://doi.org/10.1177 /001979390605900402.

43 costs the tech industry alone $16 billion per year: Leonard and Levine, "The Effect of Diversity on Turnover."

43 less likely to be dismissed: Leonard and Levine, "The Effect of Diversity on Turnover."

CHAPTER 2

48 could also be considered social identities: Blake E. Ashforth and Fred Mael, "Social Identity Theory and the Organization," *Academy of Management Review* 14, no. 1 (January 1989): 20–39, https://doi .org/10.2307/258189.

52 social system, such as our workplace: Gwyn Kirk and Margo Okazawa-Rey, "Identities" and "Social Locations." *American Identities: An Introductory Textbook* (New York and Oxford: Blackwell, 2006).

53 the ways in which they do: Peter Berger, *Invitation to Sociology: A Humanistic Perspective* (New York: Anchor Publishers, 1963).

53 we have more or less power and privilege: Gwyn Kirk and Margo Okazawa-Rey, "Identities and Social Locations: Who Am I? Who Are My People?" in *Women's Lives: Multicultural Perspectives*, 3rd ed. (New York: McGraw-Hill, 2003).

56 mental and physical health problems: Sarah A. Burgard and Katherine Y. Lin, "Bad Jobs, Bad Health? How Work and Working Conditions Contribute to Health Disparities," *American Behavioral Scientist* 57, no. 8 (August 2013): 1105–27, https://doi.org/10.1177 /0002764213487347.

57 **theory to explain the bases of social power:** John R. P. French Jr. and Bertram Raven, "The Bases of Social Power," in *Studies in Social Power*, ed. Dorwin Cartwright (Ann Arbor: Research Center for Group Dynamics, Institute for Social Research, University of Michigan, 1959).

58 **Nike's sales jumped 10 percent:** Soo Youn, "Nike Sales Booming After Colin Kaepernick Ad, Invalidating Critics," ABC News, December 21, 2018, https://abcnews.go.com/Business/nike-sales -booming-kaepernick-ad-invalidating-critics/story?id=59957137.

59 **penalized for advocating for diversity at work:** Stefanie K. Johnson and Davis R. Hekman, "Women and Minorities Are Penalized for Promoting Diversity," *Harvard Business Review*, March 23, 2016, https://hbr.org/2016/03/women-and-minorities-are-penalized-for -promoting-diversity.

62 **US civil rights movement leveraged the threat:** Azza Salama Layton, "International Pressure and the U.S. Government's Response to Little Rock," *Arkansas Historical Quarterly* 56, no. 3, 40th Anniversary of the Little Rock School Crisis (Autumn 1997): 257–72, https://doi.org/10.2307/40023174.

62 **the deciding factor in *Brown v. Board of Education*:** Justin Driver, "Rethinking the Interest-Convergence Thesis," *Northwestern University Law Review* 105, no. 1 (2015): 149–97, https://scholarlycom mons.law.northwestern.edu/nulr/vol105/iss1/3.

CHAPTER 3

71 **union membership had dropped to 6.7 percent:** Michael J. Wright, "The Decline of American Unions Is a Threat to Public Health," *American Journal of Public Health* 106, no. 6 (June 2016): 968–69, https://doi.org/10.2105/AJPH.2016.303217.

71 **one in ten workers belongs to a union:** Eli Rosenberg, "Workers Are Fired Up. But Union Participation Is Still on the Decline, New Statistics Show," *Washington Post*, January 23, 2020, https://www .washingtonpost.com/business/2020/01/22/workers-are-fired -up-union-participation-is-still-decline-new-statistics-show/.

72 the same voting rights as English workers: Frank Grizzard Jr. and D. Boyd Smith, *Jamestown Colony: A Political, Social, and Cultural History* (Santa Barbara, CA: ABC-CLIO, Inc., 2007).

73 increased wages for nearly 22 million workers nationwide: Sheila Mc-Clear, "The Future for Labor: A New Book Heralds Workers Fighting for a Fair Deal—Even When They Can't Join Unions," *New Republic*, August 20, 2019, https://newrepublic.com/article/154810/future-labor.

73 in the workplace and society at large: Steven Greenhouse, *Beaten Down, Worked Up: The Past, Present, and Future of American Labor* (New York: Alfred A. Knopf, 2019), 257.

83 George Lakey calls the "spectrum of allies": Martin Oppenheimer and George Lakey, *A Manual for Direct Action: Strategy and Tactics for Civil Rights and All Other Nonviolent Protest Movements* (Chicago: Quadrangle Books, 1965).

85 Spectrum of Allies: Josh Kahn, *Spectrum of Allies*, The Commons Social Change Library, https://commonslibrary.org/spectrum-of-allies/.

CHAPTER 4

96 some respond by rationalizing it away: Anli Yue Zhou and Paul Baker, "Confounding Factors in Using Upward Feedback to Assess the Quality of Medical Training: A Systematic Review," *Journal of Educational Evaluation for Health Professions* 11, no. 17 (August 13, 2014), https://doi.org/10.3352/jeehp.2014.11.17.

97 even being around other races: Sophie Trawalter and Jennifer A. Richeson, "Let's Talk About Race, Baby! When Whites' and Blacks' Interracial Contact Experiences Diverge," *Journal of Experimental Social Psychology* 44, no. 4 (July 2008): 1214–17, https://doi.org/10.1016/j.jesp.2008.03.013.

97 personality expression, decision making, and social behavior: William R. Hathaway and Bruce W. Newton, "Neuroanatomy, Prefrontal Cortex," in StatPearls [Internet] (Treasure Island, FL: StatPearls Publishing, 2021), last updated August 22, 2020, available from https://www.ncbi.nlm.nih.gov/books/NBK499919/.

97 **To combat the effects of cortisol, you have to prepare:** Nicklas Balboa and Richard D. Glaser, "The Neuroscience of Conversations: A Deep Dive into the Fascinating World of Conversations," *Psychology Today*, May 16, 2019, https://www.psychologytoday.com/us/blog/conversational-intelligence/201905/the-neuroscience-conversations.

98 **Scholars have been pushing it since the 1990s:** Taylor H. Cox and Stacy Blake, "Managing Cultural Diversity: Implications for Organizational Competitiveness," *The Executive* 5, no. 3 (August 1991): 45–56, http://www.jstor.org/stable/4165021.

98 **organizations perform better over time:** Michelle Kim, "Compilation of Diversity and Inclusion 'Business Case' Research Data," *Awaken* (blog), March 26, 2018, https://medium.com/awaken-blog/compilation-of-diversity-inclusion-business-case-research-data-62a471fc4a42.

99 **That's the GDP of a small European country:** Level Playing Field Institute, *The Corporate Leavers Survey: The Cost of Employee Turnover Due Solely to Unfairness in the Workplace* (San Francisco: Korn/Ferry International, 2007), https://www.smash.org/wp-content/uploads/2015/05/corporate-leavers-survey.pdf.

100 **threaten their own performance:** Jamillah Bowman Williams, "Breaking Down Bias: Legal Mandates vs. Corporate Interests," *Washington Law Review* 92 (2017): 1473–1513, https://scholarship.law.georgetown.edu/facpub/1961.

104 **$125,000 to defend an employee lawsuit:** Marissa Levin, "5 Things Companies Should Do Now to Avoid Costly (and Harmful) Employee Lawsuits," *Inc.*, December 7, 2016, https://www.inc.com/marissa-levin/5-things-employers-can-do-now-to-avoid-costly-and-harmful-employee-lawsuits.html

105 **the effectiveness of the case overall is mixed:** Bowman Williams, "Breaking Down Bias."

105 **like affirmative action, have had some success:** Harry Holzer and David Neumark, "Assessing Affirmative Action," National Bureau of Economic Research, Working Paper 7323, August 1999, 37, https://www.nber.org/papers/w7323.pdf.

106 women of color, particularly Black women: Charlie Warzel, "'A Honeypot for Assholes': Inside Twitter's 10-Year Failure to Stop Harassment," *Buzzfeed News,* August 11, 2016, https://www.buzzfeed news.com/article/charliewarzel/a-honeypot-for-assholes-inside -twitters-10-year-failure-to-s.

107 "That's not your role": Selina Wang, "Twitter Sidestepped Russian Account Warnings, Former Worker Says," *Bloomberg Technology,* November 3, 2017, https://www.bloomberg.com/news/articles /2017-11-03/former-twitter-employee-says-fake-russian-accounts -were-not-taken-seriously.

107 the outcome of the presidential election: Jon Swaine, "Twitter Admits Far More Russian Bots Posted on Election Than It Had Disclosed," *The Guardian,* January 19, 2018, https://www.theguardian .com/technology/2018/jan/19/twitter-admits-far-more-russian -bots-posted-on-election-than-it-had-disclosed.

108 criminal justice system, in hiring processes: Andrew Lee Park, "Injustice Ex Machina: Predictive Algorithms in Criminal Sentencing," Law Meets World, *UCLA Law Review,* February 19, 2019, https:// www.uclalawreview.org/injustice-ex-machina-predictive -algorithms-in-criminal-sentencing/; Jeffrey Dastin, "Amazon Scraps Secret AI Recruiting Tool That Showed Bias Against Women," Reuters, October 10, 2018, https://www.reuters.com/article/us-amazon -com-jobs-automation-insight/amazon-scraps-secret-ai -recruiting-tool-that-showed-bias-against-women-idUSKCN1 MK08G.

108 sexual abuse of Haitian earthquake survivors by its staff: Lizzie Roberts, "Oxfam Marked by 'Racism, Colonial Behaviour and Bullying Behaviours,' Report into Sexual Misconduct Scandal Finds," *The Independent,* January 16, 2019, https://www.independent.co.uk /news/world/oxfam-sexual-misconduct-scandal-report-haiti -racism-bullying-colonial-behaviours-a8731831.html.

108 accusing the organization of institutional racism: Karen McVeigh, "MSF Ran 'White Saviour' TV Ad Despite Staff Warnings over Racism," *The Guardian*, September 10, 2020, https://www.theguardian

.com/global-development/2020/sep/10/msf-ran-white-saviour -tv-ad-despite-staff-warnings-over-racism.

108 up to 40 percent in aggregate productivity and output: Lisa D. Cook, "Racism Impoverishes the Whole Economy," *New York Times*, November 18, 2020, https://www.nytimes.com/2020/11/18/business /racism-impoverishes-the-whole-economy.html.

109 not accounting for the full cost of racism: Dana M. Peterson and Catherine L. Mann, *Closing the Racial Inequality Gaps: The Economic Cost of Black Inequality in the U.S.*, *Citi GPS: Global Perspectives & Solutions*, September 2020, https://ir.citi.com/NvIUklHPi lz14Hwd3oxqZBLMn1_XPqo5FrxsZD0x6hhil84ZxaxEuJUWmak 51UHvYk75VKeHCMI%3D.

109 teaching them to fear or blame: Diane J. Goodman, *Promoting Diversity and Social Justice: Educating People from Privileged Groups*, 2nd ed., Teaching/Learning Social Justice (New York: Routledge, 2011).

110 goals while in a difficult conversation: Kerry Patterson, Joseph Grenny, Ron McMillan, and Al Switzer, *Crucial Conversations: Tools for Talking When Stakes Are High* (New York: McGraw-Hill Education, 2002), 33.

110 "What do I really want for this relationship?": Patterson, Grenny, McMillan, and Switzler, *Crucial Conversations*, 43.

CHAPTER 5

130 enough to diminish attention and impede performance: Bill Thornton, Alyson Faires, Maija Robbins, and Eric Rollins, "The Mere Presence of a Cell Phone May Be Distracting: Implications for Attention and Task Performance," *Social Psychology* 45, no. 6 (November 2014): 479–88, https://doi.org/10.1027/1864-9335/a000216.

132 numbers of Black and Brown workers have stagnated or decreased: Buck Gee and Denise Peck, *The Illusion of Asian Success: Scant Progress for Minorities in Cracking the Glass Ceiling from 2007– 2015* (New York: Ascend Foundation, 2017), https://www.ascend leadershipfoundation.org/research/the-illusion-of-asian-success.

134 **even if the impact of both actions is the same:** Melanie Tannenbaum, "'But I Didn't Mean It!' Why It's So Hard to Prioritize Impacts Over Intents," *PsySociety* (blog), *Scientific American*, October 14, 2013, https://blogs.scientificamerican.com/psysociety/e2809cbut-i-didne28099t-mean-ite2809d-why-ite28099s-so-hard-to-prioritize-impacts-over-intents/.

136 **it is in their best interest to support the advancement:** Derrick A. Bell Jr., "*Brown v. Board of Education* and the Interest-Convergence Dilemma," *Harvard Law Review* 93 (1980): 518–33, https://harvardlawreview.org/wp-content/uploads/1980/01/518-533_Online.pdf.

CHAPTER 6

153 **was fired within days:** Zoe Schiffer, "Google's Ethical AI Researchers Complained of Harassment Long Before Timnit Gebru's Firing," *The Verge*, April 21, 2021, https://www.theverge.com/2021/4/21/22396112/google-ethical-ai-team-bias-harassment-timnit-gebru-firing.

153 **committed to a psychiatric hospital:** Cassis DaCosta, "A Cards Against Humanity Writer Called Out Racism at Work. He Ended Up Institutionalized Against His Will," *Daily Beast*, August 4, 2020, https://www.thedailybeast.com/a-cards-against-humanity-writer-called-out-racism-at-work-he-ended-up-institutionalized-against-his-will.

154 **federal programs designed to legislate equality:** Carol Anderson, *White Rage: The Unspoken Truth of Our Racial Divide* (New York: Bloomsbury Publishing, 2016), 98.

155 **in order to justify their actions:** L. Taylor Phillips and Brian S. Lowery, "The Hard-Knock Life? Whites Claim Hardships in Response to Racial Inequity," *Journal of Experimental Social Psychology* 61 (November 2015): 12–18, https://doi.org/10.1016/j.jesp.2015.06.008.

159 **self-affirmation can reduce defensiveness and even prejudice:** Phillips and Lowery, "The Hard-Knock Life."

167 **they are more apathetic in the face of racism:** Margaret Hagerman, "Are Today's White Kids Less Racist Than Their Grandparents?" *The Conversation*, September 17, 2018, https://theconversation.com /are-todays-white-kids-less-racist-than-their-grandparents-101710.

170 **those with a genuine desire to learn:** Amy Johnson, "The Multiple Harms of Sea Lions," in *Perspectives on Harmful Speech Online: A Collection of Essays* (Cambridge, MA: Harvard University, 2017), https://cyber.harvard.edu/sites/cyber.harvard.edu/files/2017-08 _harmfulspeech.pdf.

174 **75 percent of people who spoke out against harassment experienced retaliation:** Tara Golshan, "Study Finds 75 Percent of Workplace Harassment Victims Experienced Retaliation When They Spoke Up," *Vox*, October 15, 2017, https://www.vox.com/identities/2017 /10/15/16438750/weinstein-sexual-harassment-facts.

175 **the number of workers and workforce complaints has increased:** Maryam Jameel, "More and More Workplace Discrimination Cases are Being Closed Before They're Even Investigated," *Vox*, June 14, 2019, https://www.vox.com/identities/2019/6/14/18663296 /congress-eeoc-workplace-discrimination.

176 **just ask the Google walkout organizers:** Alex Press, "Women are Filing More Harassment Claims in the #MeToo Era. They're Also Facing More Retaliation," *Vox*, May 9, 2019, https://www.vox.com /the-big-idea/2019/5/9/18541982/sexual-harassment me too eeoc -complaints.

CHAPTER 7

180 **even acquire an interest in its maintenance:** Charles Tilly, *Durable Inequality* (Berkeley: University of California Press, 1999), 96.

181 **and cement hatred and bigotry:** Ibram X. Kendi, *Stamped from the Beginning: The Definitive History of Racist Ideas in America* (New York: Bold Type Books, 2017).

184 **"they have morality on their side":** Michael Young, "Down with Meritocracy," *The Guardian*, June 28, 2001, https://www.theguardian .com/politics/2001/jun/29/comment.

184 only 31 percent of White students do: Emma Garcia, "Schools Are Still Segregated and Black Children Are Paying a Price," Economic Policy Institute, February 12, 2020, https://www.epi.org/publica tion/schools-are-still-segregated-and-black-children-are -paying-a-price/.

184 more than 25 percent in the last ten years: Abigail Johnson Hess, "The Cost of College Increased by More Than 25% in the Last 10 Years—Here's Why," CNBC, December 13, 2019, https://www.cnbc.com /2019/12/13/cost-of-college-increased-by-more-than-25percent -in-the-last-10-years.html.

185 or the children of donors or faculty: Jordan Weissmann, "43 Percent of White Students Harvard Admits Are Legacies, Jocks, or the Kids of Donors and Faculty," *Slate*, September 23, 2019, https:// slate.com/business/2019/09/harvard-admissions-affirmative -action-white-students-legacy-athletes-donors.html.

185 White male prospective grad students than any other demographic: Katherine L. Milkman, Modupe Akinola, and Dolly Chugh, "What Happens Before? A Field Experiment Exploring How Pay and Representation Differentially Shape Bias on the Pathway into Organizations," *Journal of Applied Psychology* 100, no. 6 (November 2015): 1678–1712, https://doi.org/10.1037/apl0000022.

185 with whom they discuss important matters are White: Daniel Cox, Juhem Navarro-Rivera, and Robert P. Jones, "Race, Religion, and Political Affiliation of Americans' Core Social Networks," PRRI, August 3, 2016, https://www.prri.org/research/poll-race-religion -politics-americans-social-networks/.

185 most biased outcomes in hiring and performance evaluation: Marianne Cooper, "The False Promise of Meritocracy," *The Atlantic*, Business, December 1, 2015, https://www.theatlantic.com/business /archive/2015/12/meritocracy/418074/.

186 really poor predictors of future performance: Noam Shpancer, "Poor Predictors: Job Interviews Are Useless and Unfair," *Psychology Today*, August 31, 2020, https://www.psychologytoday.com/intl /blog/insight-therapy/202008/poor-predictors-job-interviews -are-useless-and-unfair; Dave Heller, "Work Experience Poor Pre-

dictor of Future Job Performance," Florida State University College of Business, June 2, 2019, https://business.fsu.edu/article/work-experience-poor-predictor-future-job-performance.

189 "selection for training, including apprenticeship": John F. Kennedy, "Executive Order 10925—Establishing the President's Committee on Equal Employment Opportunity," online by Gerhard Peters and John T. Woolley, *The American Presidency Project*, https://www.presidency.ucsb.edu/node/237176.

190 no longer bound by affirmative action requirements: Jonathan S. Leonard, "The Impact of Affirmative Action on Employment," *Journal of Labor Economics* 2, no. 4 (October 1984): 439–63, https://www.jstor.org/stable/2534808; Jonathan S. Leonard, "The Effectiveness of Equal Employment Law and Affirmative Action Regulation," National Bureau of Economic Research, Working Paper 1745, November 1985, https://www.nber.org/system/files/working_papers/w1745/w1745.pdf.

191 perform just as well on the job as their peers: Harry Holzer and David Neumark, "Are Affirmative Action Hires Less Qualified? Evidence from Employer-Employee Data on New Hires," *Journal of Labor Economics* 17, no. 3 (July 1999): 534–69, https://doi.org/10.1086/209930.

191 nearly 70 percent of Asian Americans support affirmative action: Kimmy Yam, "70% of Asian Americans Support Affirmative Action. Here's Why Misperceptions Exist," NBC News, November 14, 2020, https://www.nbcnews.com/news/asian-america/70-asian-americans-support-affirmative-action-here-s-why-misconceptions-n1247806.

191 beneficiaries of workplace affirmative action programs: Rob Mank, "Men Far More Likely to Benefit from Affirmative Action in College Admissions," CBS News, September 26, 2011, https://www.cbsnews.com/news/men-far-more-likely-to-benefit-from-affirmative-action-in-college-admissions/.

191 designed to maintain an equal gender ratio: Nick Anderson, "The Gender Factor in College Admissions: Do Men or Women Have an Edge?" *Washington Post*, March 26, 2014, https://www.washing

tonpost.com/local/education/the-gender-factor-in-college-admis
sions/2014/03/26/4996e988-b4e6-11e3-8020-b2d790b3c9e1
_story.html.

192 when it specifically benefits Black people: Faye J. Crosby, Aarti
Iyer, and Sirinda Sincharoen, "Understanding Affirmative Action,"
Annual Review of Psychology 57 (January 2006): 585–611, https://
doi.org/10.1146/annurev.psych.57.102904.190029.

192 increasing their estimation of their own competence: Miguel M.
Unzueta, Brian S. Lowery, and Eric D. Knowles, "How Believing in
Affirmative Action Quotas Protects White Men's Self-Esteem," *Organizational Behavior and Human Decision Processes* 105, no. 1
(2007): 1–13, https://doi.org/ 10.1016/j.obhdp.2007.05.001.

192 makes them feel better about themselves: Miguel M. Unzueta, An-
gélica S. Gutiérrez, and Negin Ghavami, "How Believing in Affirmative Action Quotas Affects White Women's Self-Image," *Journal
of Experimental Social Psychology* 46, no. 1 (January 2010): 120–26,
https://doi.org/10.1016/j.jesp.2009.08.017.

195 from a measly 0.7 percent to 0.4 percent: *ABA Profile of the Legal
Profession*, American Bar Association, July 2020, 33, https://www
.americanbar.org/content/dam/aba/administrative/news/2020/07
/potlp2020.pdf.

195 representation in professional and managerial roles: US Equal Employment Opportunity Commission, *American Experiences versus
American Expectations* (Washington, DC: Equal Employment Opportunity Commission, July 2015), https://www.eeoc.gov/special
-report/american-experiences-versus-american-expectations.

196 55 percent and 350 percent, respectively: Collin West, Gopinath
Sundaramurthy, and Marlon Nichols, "Deconstructing the Pipeline
Myth and the Case for More Diverse Fund Managers," *Kauffman
Fellows* (blog), February 4, 2020, https://www.kauffmanfellows.org
/journal_posts/the-pipeline-myth-ethnicity-fund-managers.

196 around 3 percent Latino and 1 percent Black: Quoctrung Bui and
Claire Cain Miller, "Why Tech Degrees Are Not Putting More Blacks
and Hispanics into Tech Jobs," *The Upshot* (blog), *New York Times*,

February 25, 2016, https://www.nytimes.com/2016/02/26/upshot/dont-blame-recruiting-pipeline-for-lack-of-diversity-in-tech.html.

196 10 percent of computer science grads are Latino and 9 percent are Black: "Bachelor's Degrees Earned by African Americans, by Major," American Physical Society, https://www.aps.org/programs/education/statistics/aamajors.cfm; "Bachelor's Degrees Earned by Hispanics, by Major," American Physical Society, https://www.aps.org/programs/education/statistics/hispanicmajors.cfm.

196 17 percent less than White law students: National Association for Law Placement, Inc., "NALP's New Employment and Salary Report Highlights Disparities in Outcomes by Race and Ethnicity," press release, October 21, 2020, https://www.nalp.org/uploads/PressReleases/NALPPressReleaseJobsandJDsOctober212020.pdf.

197 and to receive benefits at the jobs they do hold: Ariana De La Fuente and Marissa Alayna Navarro, "Black and Latinx Students Are Getting Less Bang for Their Bachelor's Degrees," Center for American Progress, January 23, 2020, https://www.americanprogress.org/issues/education-postsecondary/news/2020/01/23/479692/black-latinx-students-getting-less-bang-bachelors-degrees/.

197 Every other group is drastically underrepresented: *A Rising Tide of Hate and Violence Against Asian Americans in New York During COVID-19: Impact, Causes, Solutions* (New York: Asian American Bar Association and Paul, Weiss, Rifkind, Wharton & Garrison LLP, 2021), https://cdn.ymaws.com/www.aabany.org/resource/resmgr/press_releases/2021/A_Rising_Tide_of_Hate_and_Vi.pdf.

201 worse outcomes for their Black and Brown employees: Buck Gee and Denise Peck, "The Illusion of Asian Success: Scant Progress for Minorities in Cracking the Glass Ceiling from 2007–2015," Ascend: Pan-Asian Leaders, October 2017, http://aapidata.com/wp-content/uploads/2017/10/TheIllusionofAsianSuccess.pdf.

201 prestigious spaces like technology, law, medicine, and finance: Jennifer Cheeseman, "Number of Women Lawyers at Record High But Men Still Highest Earners," *America Counts* (blog), US Census Bu-

reau, May 8, 2018, https://www.census.gov/library/stories/2018/05/women-lawyers.html.

201 **female representation has also increased in leadership roles:** "The State of Women in Corporate America," LeanIn.org, accessed July 12, 2021, https://leanin.org/women-in-the-workplace-2019.

202 **number of Black employees has hovered steadily at less than 2 percent:** Maxine Williams, "Facebook 2020 Diversity Report: Advancing Opportunity for All," Facebook Newsroom, July 15, 2020, https://about.fb.com/news/2020/07/facebook-2020-diversity-report/.

202 **only one in twenty-five were women of color:** Rachel Thomas et al., *Women in the Workplace: 2019,* Lean In and McKinsey & Company, https://womenintheworkplace.com/2019.

202 **representation for people of color at those levels declined:** Asian American Bar Association and Paul, Weiss, *A Rising Tide of Hate and Violence.*

202 **support from their managers and colleagues:** Sarah Coury et al., *Women in the Workplace: 2020,* Lean In and McKinsey & Company, https://www.mckinsey.com/featured-insights/diversity-and-inclusion/women-in-the-workplace.

206 **foreign workers report discrimination in the workplace:** Songmi Woo, "Japanese Companies Confront Reality of Racial Harassment," *Kyodo News,* February 7, 2020, https://english.kyodonews.net/news/2020/02/f2a11c7173d3-feature-japanese-companies-confront-reality-of-racial-harassment.html.

207 **44.9 billion Australian dollars between 2001 and 2011:** Joseph Losavio, "What Racism Costs Us All," *Finance & Development,* September 2020, https://www.imf.org/external/pubs/ft/fandd/2020/09/pdf/the-economic-cost-of-racism-losavio.pdf.

207 **racial naivete and inexperience with societal diversity:** Motoko Rich and Hikari Hida, "In Japan, the Message of Anti-Racism Protests Fails to Hit Home," *New York Times,* July 1, 2020, https://www.nytimes.com/2020/07/01/world/asia/japan-racism-black-lives-matter.html.

207 **impedes movements for racial justice:** Sharon Stanley, "The Persistence of Myth: Brazil's Undead 'Racial Democracy,'" *Contem-*

porary Political Theory (2021), https://doi.org/10.1057/s41296-021 -00477-x.

CHAPTER 8

210 **providing information alone is not enough:** Jesse Singal, "Awareness is Overrated," *The Cut* (blog), *New York*, July 17, 2014, https:// www.thecut.com/2014/07/awareness-is-overrated.html.

210 **the awareness of bad behavior normalized it:** Robert B. Cialdini et al., "Managing Social Norms for Persuasive Impact," *Social Influence* 1, no. 1 (2006): 3–15, https://doi.org/10.1080/15534510500181459.

211 **faster to measure the quantity and quality of talk:** Jeffrey Pfeffer and Robert I. Sutton, *The Knowing Doing Gap* (Cambridge: Harvard Business School Press, 2000), https://homepages.se.edu/cvon bergen/files/2012/12/The-Knowing-Doing-Gap2.pdf.

219 **on average 11.6 percent more than those who don't:** Courtney Connley, "Report: The Race and Gender of Your Office 'Sponsor' Can Affect Your Salary," CNBC, September 9, 2019, https://www.cnbc .com/2019/09/09/the-race-and-gender-of-your-office-sponsor -can-affect-your-salary.html.

220 **because men have more power within organizations:** David Smith and Brad Johnson, "When Men Mentor Women," *HBR IdeaCast* (podcast), episode 653, 2018, https://hbr.org/podcast/2018/10/when -men-mentor-women.

220 **make less than those with White ones:** Connley, "Report: The Race and Gender of Your Office 'Sponsor' Can Affect Your Salary."

223 **Access to information can decrease these gaps:** Marc-David L. Seidel, Jeffrey T. Polzer, and Katherine J. Stewart, "Friends in High Places: The Effects of Social Networks on Discrimination in Salary Negotiations," *Administrative Science Quarterly* 45, no. 1 (March 2000): 1–24, https://doi.org/10.2307/2666977.

223 **more than 90 percent of Fortune 500:** Judi C. Casey, "Employee Resource Groups: A Strategic Business Resource for Today's Workplace," Executive Briefing Series, Boston College Center for Work and Family, no date, https://www.bc.edu/content/dam/files/centers

/cwf/research/publications3/executivebriefingseries-2/Executive
Briefing_EmployeeResourceGroups.pdf.

228 **disproportionately harms Black and Brown communities:** Hiroko
Tabuchi and Nadja Popovich, "People of Color Breathe More Haz-
ardous Air. The Sources Are Everywhere," *New York Times*, April 28,
2021, https://www.nytimes.com/2021/04/28/climate/air-pollution
-minorities.html.

228 **access to benefits like healthcare in states like California:** Tina Bel-
lon, "Uber, Lyft Have a California Playbook to Fight Proposed U.S.
Rules on Workers," Reuters, May 3, 2021, https://www.reuters.com
/technology/uber-lyft-have-california-playbook-fight-proposed
-us-rules-workers-2021-05-03/.

231 **"The diversity of our voices makes us stronger":** "Mission Statement,"
Alphabet Workers Union, accessed July 13, 2021, https://alphabetwork
ersunion.org/principles/mission-statement/.

232 **to find the union that might be the right fit:** "Our Affiliated Unions,"
AFL-CIO, accessed July 13, 2021, https://aflcio.org/about/our-unions
-and-allies/our-affiliated-unions.

233–234 **bias, like training, don't really work:** Frank Dobbin and Alexandra
Kalev, "Why Diversity Programs Fail," *Harvard Business Review*,
July–August 2016, https://hbr.org/2016/07/why-diversity-programs
-fail.

CHAPTER 9

238 **because of toxicity in the workplace:** "The High Cost of a Toxic
Workplace Culture: How Culture Impacts the Workforce—And the
Bottom Line," Society for Human Resource Management, 2019,
https://pages.shrm.org/2019culturereport.

239 **more than 95 percent:** Jessica Dickler, "'Great Resignation' Gains
Steam as Return-to-Work Plans Take Effect," CNBC, June 29, 2021,
https://www.cnbc.com/2021/06/29/more-people-plan-to-quit
-as-return-to-work-plans-go-into-effect-.html.

247 **the American workforce is bound by nondisclosure agreements:**
Randall S. Thomas and Norman D. Bishara, and Kenneth J. Martin,
"An Empirical Analysis of Non-Competition Clauses and Other

Restrictive Post-Employment Covenants," *Vanderbilt Law Review*, vol. 68, no. 1 (2015), Vanderbilt Law and Economics Research Paper No. 14-11, SSRN: https://ssrn.com/abstract=2401781 or http://dx .doi.org/10.2139/ssrn.2401781.

CONCLUSION

263 **depression, lowered self-esteem, anxiety, and sleeplessness:** Sabrina Barr, "Six Ways Social Media Affects Your Mental Health," *The Independent*, October 7, 2020, https://www.independent.co.uk/life -style/health-and-families/social-media-mental-health-negative -effects-depression-anxiety-addiction-memory-a8307196.html.

263 **compounded by the vicarious trauma:** Julia Naftulin, "Police Brutality Imagery on Social Media Can Cause Lasting Trauma, Especially for Black People," *Insider,* June 3, 2020, https://www.insider .com/police-brutality-imagery-social-media-trauma-mental-health -2020-6.

264 **just 4 percent of therapists in the US are Black:** Luona Lin, Karen Stamm, and Peggy Christidis, "Datapoint: How Diverse Is the Psychology Workforce?" *Monitor on Psychology* 18, no. 2 (February 2018), https://www.apa.org/monitor/2018/02/datapoint.